STREETWISE
INVESTING
IN
RENTAL
HOUSING

A Detailed Strategy
for Financial Independence

by
H. Roger Neal

Panoply Press, Incorporated
Lake Oswego, Oregon

Copyright © 1994, 1996, 1997 by H. Roger Neal
Latest update: 1997

Printed in the United States of America

Cover design: Bruce DeRoos
Cover & text illustrations: Janora Bayot

Library of Congress Cataloging-in-Publication Data
Neal, H. Roger
     Streetwise investing in rental housing : a detailed strategy for financial independence / by H. Roger Neal.
          p.   cm.
     Includes index.
     ISBN 1-882877-03-9 : $15.95
     1. Rental housing.   2. Real estate investment.
     3. Real estate management. I. Title.
     HD1394.N4   1994
     332.63'243—dc20   93-32874
                                                                        CIP

PANOPLY PRESS, INC.
P. O. Box 1885
Lake Oswego, Oregon 97035
(503) 697-7964   (800) 826-6579

Publisher's catalog is available upon request.

Acknowledgments

My special thanks to Lee Jewell, my acquisition editor, who appreciated a realistic approach toward financial independence. And to my son Roger for his computer expertise. To my brother John for his encouragement and legal counsel. And to Bruce DeRoos and Janora Bayot for their superior cover design and illustrations.

Any form of real estate investment involves an element of risk. While the whole purpose of my investment strategy is to minimize that risk while maximizing the income received from rental properties, it is important that you, as an investor, recognize the pitfalls and guard against them. Rely on expert advice from your team of professionals: your attorney, accountant, tax advisor and real estate agent. Although the information contained in this book has been edited with great care, changes or revisions in laws, tax rules, financing guidelines and real estate practices occur and regional variations exist. Take time to be a well-informed investor.

A Note About The Case Histories:
In this book, you'll find true case histories describing situations I have encountered in my years as an investor. In each case, names and some identifying details have been changed to protect the privacy of the individuals involved.

To my wife, Nancy, and children, Robert, Jenny, Roger, Katelyn, and Audrey whose inspiration, support, and sacrifice facilitated my success.

TABLE OF CONTENTS

Part III   ACQUIRING PROPERTIES

Chapter 5   Financing Your Properties. 65

Chapter 6   Closing the Transaction. 83

Part IV   IMPROVING AND MAINTAINING
YOUR INVESTMENTS

Part V   MANAGING YOUR RENTALS

Chapter 9   Renting Your Units 127

Chapter 10 Managing Difficult Tenants 149

Part VI   THE BUSINESS OF INVESTING

Chapter 11 Setting Up Your Office 173

Part VII   SELLING AND EXCHANGING
            PROPERTIES

Chapter 12 Selling 187

Preface

Years ago, when I first decided that I wanted to be a real estate investor, with a large portfolio of rental property, I can recall my father reminding me that I had never fixed anything correctly in my life. In fact, he was quick to point out that I had even stripped my bicycle pedal while trying to reattach it. Furthermore, I stripped everything with threads whenever I applied a wrench. So how could I possibly expect to handle the day-to-day demands of investment property?

Admittedly, there was some justification for my father's opinion. But I was sure I'd left all my thread-stripping childhood days behind me. Since then, I had served in the Army for three years and was now an adult. I knew that the high financial goals I'd set for myself were easily within my reach, and real estate investment seemed to be the quickest, easiest route to take.

So against my father's better judgment, I invested in rental property and became a landlord. My goal was similar to that of so many other landlords: I collected the rent, and tried hard not to fix anything. But after years of low rents and incessant repair calls, I was certainly no closer to my goal. I decided that if I were to succeed, I needed a different plan. My income was insufficient, and I was easily frustrated with the tenants. So I decided to turn my back on real estate and look for other opportunities.

I searched endlessly for just one or two small businesses to buy that would allow me to earn $15,000 to $20,000 on each. But I couldn't find one business which met this criterion. Most small businesses that I investigated yielded less than $10,000 each and would require long hours of work to make this meager income. If I paid someone to work for me, I'd be lucky to break even. I ruled out franchises because they required thousands of dollars up front just for their names and ideas.

Although I had not achieved a high level of success in rental properties on my first venture, the money, flexibility, and opportunity lured me back to the real estate business. This time I vowed to succeed. Over the next several years, I worked on developing a new real estate strategy for myself, one with a different approach and a fresh outlook. The rents I collected were much higher and I found a way to eliminate almost all of the repair calls. I became a far better landlord to my tenants. In addition, I made more money than I ever dreamed possible and actually enjoyed going to work. All I needed to do differently was **everything**! My new strategy worked for me and it can work for you. With it, my income, investment, and retirement problems were solved, as yours can be also. What keeps most investors from greater success and financial independence isn't a lack of intelligence or luck; it's the absence of a workable plan.

This book reveals all the techniques necessary to achieve maximum success in owning rental housing. In it, you'll find a detailed explanation of all phases of investment, from selection and buying, through renting, repairing and managing, to selling and running your investment business. This will be the only book that you will ever need to help you decide if real estate rentals are right for you. Once you make that decision, this book will guide you in a step-by-step process that will help you find the best solutions to your problems. I hope you will take the time to read the entire book before you invest. Even chapters covering topics you think you won't need until later contain valuable information to help you develop your own personal investment strategy.

Throughout this guide, you will find warning signs that should be heeded. If you decide to embark on this venture, you'll find that I've noted all of the typical— and not so typical— mistakes investors make. If you are now investing in income housing and are currently unsuccessful, reading this book will pinpoint your deficiencies and assist in problem solving. Your weaknesses will become strengths.

At no time, will there be overdramatization. You won't see me in a Hawaiian shirt, driving a Rolls Royce, or describing untold fortunes in real estate to sugarcoat the investment picture. Earning $100,000 to $200,000 annually or owning real estate worth one- to two-million dollars is not my idea of untold fortunes. However, it is precisely my idea of the financial independence that can easily be acquired by creating and owning your own business.

In this book, there will be no promise of "instant cash." What you will find instead is the real world of real estate, with real problems and real work. The income which you will find depicted will be a realistic return on your investment. Actual investments that I have made will be carefully outlined for your scrutiny and analysis.

This real estate investment guide offers an excellent strategy for those who wish to invest $3,000 or more, while maximizing their investment potential and profitability. It would be fair to mention, however, that all investments involve risks, and this is certainly no exception. With most investments, as the return increases, so do the risks. But I haven't found this to be the case with the methods I use. It has been important to me, as an investor, to minimize risks and to develop a successful, money-making, full-time, self-made business that allows me to be financially independent. This book aids in reducing those risks and maximizing income.

It is no surprise to anyone that most new businesses fail. Furthermore, it is also a fact that it generally takes years for new businesses to even show a profit. Unlike other businesses, real estate can make money the first month after acquisition. I consider each property a "part-time job." If you want more money, just buy another part-time job. Before long, you have many part-time jobs that add up to executive-level income. Don't forget the other positive aspects about the business of real estate investment: you name your own hours and dictate your own pay raises by raising the rents when the market allows.

The properties I have found to be most profitable are not in high-rent neighborhoods. My best returns come from three-bedroom, side-by-side duplexes (or "doubles" as they are often called to differentiate them from upstairs-downstairs duplexes) in lower-priced areas. Upscale rentals could never yield the cash flow found in these neighborhoods. Using the strategy in this book, your goal will be to establish a large base income by investing in a portfolio of twenty doubles. Once established, you can continue with this pattern or branch out to large apartment complexes, small businesses, or other investments.

If you have never invested in real estate, but are eager to try and have money to invest, this book will give you the support and encouragment you will need to develop a profitable business. If, on the other hand you are already investing and have achieved some level of success, this book will help you fine-tune your method of operation and enable your business to run smoothly and more profitably.

Let the adventure begin!

Part I
Establishing
Goals & Strategy

1

Establish Your Investment Goals

Y ou've seen it on television many times, perhaps on one of the late-night shows, advertising expensive real estate tapes and books that are sure to make you rich. A millionaire, of both national and international renown, is shown with elaborate houses, cars and, let's not forget, beautiful women in the background. This individual tells of his early beginnings, his initial poverty and later bankruptcy. Since his rocky start is far worse than your present situation, this, of course, gives you hope and confidence. It leads you to think that if this person can become a millionaire, you can as well.

Keep watching and you'll learn that his wealth was all earned in the real estate business, through investment in housing. While my career and income are proof of the fact that real estate investment can be very profitable, it is the actual steps which he advises you to take that concern me. Were these investments made with the high-risk tactics presented on the show? I think not. In this book, I'll show you a better way.

Here are the facts. Nearly everyone I've ever known who has dabbled in real estate investment has ultimately failed. Very few have survived the fallout and have made a successful career in real estate investment. Yet early in their careers, the majority of the investors I've met appeared to be doing quite well. I've watched them purchase large apartment buildings of twelve units or more and have seen them drive expensive cars. Invariably, I would listen to tales about them leaving the closing table with big checks. On a recent television show, I watched a husband and wife team state that on their first property alone they left the closing with a $100,000 check! (I'll tell you more about them in Chapter 2.) Naturally, most of us would envy them. In fact, testimonials like these often made me wonder if I should adopt their techniques.

But why is there such an unusually high percentage of failure in rental housing investment? Are the investments themselves to blame, or are the techniques used by the investor at fault? After many years of investing, I came to the conclusion that the strategy of the investor, or lack of it, is the primary cause of failure. The biggest problems in investment property usually result from the wrong approach and a poor outlook, by investors with no set goals on which to stay focused.

Real estate is absolutely the best way to accumulate and increase wealth beyond your expectations. From my lengthy observation and extensive personal experience with actual real estate investments, I have developed what I consider to be the best method of investing in rental housing, and you'll find my investment strategy described in detail in this book. It does not borrow flashy ideas from the famous salesmen you see on late-night television. You'll find my concepts innovative, but you'll see that they are very basic and honest as well. In this book, you'll find the truth about real estate investment, however unglamorous that may seem at times. The traps and pitfalls are not bypassed here to glorify the investment. After reading my book, you'll realize that there are no get-rich-quick schemes. If you're willing to take the time and make the effort to become street smart in this business, you'll reap a healthy reward for the work that you have performed.

Establish Your Initial Goal

When I ask would-be investors to describe their initial goal, most people express a desire to quit their nine-to-five jobs and start their own businesses. While this dream is commendable, it's really more of a **result** than a **goal**. It is far too vague to be an effective investment objective and so does not give the direction you'll need to give your business plans focus. Instead, be more direct and explicit in your investment analysis. First, concentrate on your business venture, setting the goal of increasing its profitability until you are assured of its continual success. Then quit your current job, if that is your dream. Fortunately rental property investment is one venture which allows you to profit from this conservative approach to beginning your own business.

Your Primary Goal: Generating Income

Now back to the idea of goalsetting: specifically, your primary investment goal should be to **generate income**. Granted, an expensive house, cars and plenty of money in the bank may be desirable and attainable, but don't make the mistake of focusing your attention on these. It is difficult to make your everyday business decisions based on your wish for a dream car. Without an appropriate business goal, the dream car could easily win out over carpet for one of your investment properties.

Don't confuse cash in the bank with income that your investments are generating. As a goal, the accumulation of a hefty bank account is not the direction you should be taking. Obviously, you will always need cash for purchasing and repairing, but this is secondary to generating income. When you apply for a loan, any banker will tell you that your $100,000 or $200,000 in the bank means next to nothing. As bankers are quick to point out, "You could spend that tomorrow. What we consider is income." Sure, cash in the bank often indicates a high level of self-discipline and hard work to accumulate such a savings. But remember, what really matters is income, not cash or assets. The income generated by many rentals together will provide the cash necessary for new down payments during acquisition phases and for the leisure items later as well.

The entire investment strategy outlined in this book is based solely upon increasing your income in a very systematic method. Each property must produce to its maximum potential, thereby reducing wasted time and effort on additional buildings. In other words, your goal should be to net in one investment the income that other investors net in two. To accomplish this, you'll need to work smart and invest wisely. You must establish your complete game plan before you make your first contract offer and you must promise yourself that each unit must generate positive cash flow, or it will not be purchased. As you read through the chapters in this book, you'll learn how to formulate your game plan and then put it into practice.

2

Choosing the Right Investment Strategy

On television late one night, I watched a couple claim that they had "made" an instant $100,000 buying investment real estate. As I watched in surprise, they boasted about the new Jaguar and trip to Jamaica their rental property had paid for. Where did this $100,000 windfall come from? Since they hadn't sold the property, the check was not for earned profits from the transaction. Instead it was a loan against the equity in the property—"cash-out" financing.

Investment methods like this, which recommend buying real estate and withdrawing cash from properties have been displayed many times over by so-called "experts" on television, selling expensive books and tapes. You might easily conclude that this theory is ideal for anyone, especially in a market where there are plenty of desperate sellers. The problem, I believe, is that these procedures sound great and they are actually possible to enact, to a certain point. Consequently, investors are quick to implement them. Yet, in the long run, these creative tactics simply inhibit growth. Some of these methods are the quickest way to failure and bankruptcy in investment housing.

Take a look at the example of the married couple who received the $100,000 check at the closing table. They boasted that they made this money on the day of the closing and, because of their investment, they were now

$100,000 richer. Don't these people realize that this money must be repaid? Let's be realistic. The only way these folks would really make this amount is if they actually **sold** the property. Now, instead of owing the lender the balance on a smaller first mortgage, they now owe an additional $100,000, either on a new and larger first mortgage or on a second mortgage. Someone must repay this debt. If you asked the couple, they'd take the position that the tenants will pay it back. But this couple's names are on the note, not the tenants'. So they, the owners, will ultimately pay it back. I sincerely hope that the good time was worth it because the payback can truly be difficult.

Consider this: if there really is that much equity, why did the couple not simply sell the property and obtain the money this way? Had the couple done this, then they really would have earned this amount and would not be obligated for either note. Although I encourage you to keep all properties in your portfolio indefinitely, there are times when you need cash to enhance your buying power. If your personal savings are depleted and you need a boost, selling and cashing out on a property or two would be the wisest method to accumulate cash. This will be explained in greater detail in Chapter 12, which discusses the selling of your real estate.

Often you do have the opportunity to leave the closing table with a check. I wholly disagree with this tactic. Each equity check you receive makes your goal harder and harder to reach. (Remember your primary goal of generating income?) Perhaps if their goals were spelled out more clearly, investors would not be so quick to jump for the cash. Immediately, this tactic increases your debt and decreases your cash flow. If cash is borrowed on a building rather than allowing your equity to create an income, you may, if you're lucky, break even. Worse yet, you certainly stand a good chance of losing money, a situation that clearly restricts your growth potential. It also is the main reason investors develop that cynical attitude which is so prevalent in real estate. Breaking even or losing money definitely takes the fun out of real estate investing.

How About "Chain Investing" (Leveraging)?

In the example we've been discussing, the couple took their $100,000 check and spent it on a Jaguar and a vacation to Jamaica. Now let's look at a different scenario; let's see what happens when that equity check is reinvested in a second property.

Let us suppose for a moment that you assumed a loan on a double which nets $200 per month. You have, thereby, increased your income by $2400 per year. If you keep the existing financing in place and move on to the next investment property, you will be on the road to success by adding to the current $200 cash flow. However, you may have the opportunity to extract $10,000 in cash, for example, by refinancing or obtaining a second mortgage. On the surface, this sounds absolutely fantastic! The cash flow of $200 per month from the property will cover the monthly payment on the new loan. You now have $10,000 and the tenants will repay the debt. How tempting it is to grasp the opportunity to buy that long-awaited personal item!

Let us assume that you resist the temptation to buy a car, take a vacation, or make any other personal expenditures. Suppose that you decide to reinvest the entire $10,000 in real estate, a tactic that you'll often hear recommended on late-night television. So, eager to get on with your investment plans, you buy another double, using the $10,000 cash to cover the down payment and repairs of the second property. With this building also, you'll receive $200 in cash flow. However, remember that the first double now has a zero cash flow because the $200 that you were earning is now repaying the $10,000 note. So now you own two doubles and you net a total of $200 per month (from your second property).

As you can see, this investment chain can continue endlessly. You could easily accumulate ten doubles and net only $200 per month total. On the one hand, you can brag about how you withdrew $10,000 nine times and reinvested all of it. On the other hand, now you have ten doubles to maintain, with the expenses necessitated by repairs and routine upkeep. The minute income of $200 a month won't stretch very far. Any vacancies or major repairs will bury you quickly at this point.

As you recall, we did assume that all of the cash sums drawn from the properties were used to actually buy more properties. Imagine, however, that you withdrew $10,000 each from five properties and diverted some of the funds for major repairs on currently owned properties or spent it on yourself. Imagine spending the entire $50,000 on personal expenditures. You are not only in a precarious financial situation, trying to make ends meet, but consider this also: you're working for free because you have no cash flow. On top of that, you are so buried in mortgage balances that you may not be able to sell the properties and get out from under them. You now have little or no equity and, unfortunately, no monthly profit either.

I have used these figures only as an example. Whether you net $200, $400 or $500 per month on each property, or borrow $10,000, $15,000 or $25,000 per property, the result is the same. It is ultimately a disaster to borrow from your investment property's equity. Your primary goal of generating income will certainly not involve draining the properties of their equity and cash flow.

Perhaps when the avalanche of bills comes in the mail, you will realize that you are in deep trouble. You own all of this real estate, but you have no money and no monthly cash flow. Does this prospect appeal to you? Not to me! If I'm going to maintain ten or twenty doubles, I want to make some serious money for my efforts. Investing is not a hobby for me; I want it to pay well. This is certainly one illuminating lesson on how to go broke and develop a cynical attitude toward real estate.

Case History: Take my investment... please!

I recently purchased a double and, while working there, I noticed a van next door. Out stepped an acquaintance of mine I hadn't seen in years. When I had known him earlier, he had been a real estate broker and investor, a man who appeared to have all the trappings of a successful career. He had invested aggressively, implementing some of those high-risk ideas I've just been discussing. He explained that he was not the broker of his own firm any more, but was now working for someone else. At this particular location, his investment was a single house. He asked if I'd be interested in making an offer to buy it, so I looked at the figures.

His original purchase price was $4,000. Naturally, he invested additional repair money, but he did not divulge the amount. Upon completion, he acquired a high mortgage and cashed out on it. The balance now is $26,000— as much as the home is worth in today's market— and once again, the building is in run-down condition. The rental amount is $350 and the payment is $326. Needless to say, he was not in the best of spirits. Did I want to buy it? Of course not! I pointed out that he was buried in it and that I refuse to break even on any investment. Unhappily, he agreed that if he were to do it all over again, he would never refinance anything in order to cash out.

His lesson was a particularly hard one: he mentioned that he was buried in his other properties as well. Had he invested differently, he could have many properties paid off by now, like I do, with an excellent cash flow like mine. Because of a poor strategy, he was a slave to his investments, working for no income and feeling that he had failed miserably. Even the fancy car was gone.

Avoid Long-term Financing

Why is it that everybody wants to buy properties with nothing down and finance them for thirty years? This is absolute lunacy. Why should you pay thirty years for a property which can be paid off in eight or ten years? Frankly, I don't know. Advice like this is given regularly by other experts and accepted widely by novice investors without question. Yet in my opinion, this is another main cause for so many investment failures. The technique is incompatible with the strategy for success.

Years ago when I was a teenager, I remember when lenders increased the loan amortization schedule from fifteen to twenty years. At that time, it was a landmark opportunity for people to become homeowners. Shortly thereafter, credit cards and car loans were lengthened as well. In fact, overall credit became quite lax. It seemed that, overnight, home loans were extended to thirty years. Actually, when I bought my first home, I never gave the thirty-year loan a second thought. It allowed me to keep my payments low and buy a decent property. Then, too, most mortgage interest on principal and secondary residences was and is tax deductible. But if you are investing in rental properties, now is the time to evaluate and pursue the positive aspects of financing on a shorter term.

It's a very good idea to go back in time, to when it was frugal (and laudable) to have a short-term loan. You must fight off the temptation of easy credit. If your goal is to acquire investment properties and to get them paid off in the shortest period of time, you are obviously wise to finance them for a short term and not for thirty years. It's a good idea to encourage yourself to set limitations on the way you purchase property. The maximum length of loan to assume should be twenty years and the maximum new loan should be fifteen years, be it bank- or seller-financing. In fact, I'll go one step further and say that your primary efforts should be focused on new owner-financed loans which are under ten years. This is how you will achieve your goal quickly.

Do You Have the Necessary Financial Skills?

Recently, I heard on a local access television channel that "bankruptcy doesn't matter." Granted, if you have declared bankruptcy, you can still buy investment properties through methods that I and many others describe. But frankly, I am appalled at the idea that bankruptcy is of little concern. If you have had difficulty in managing your personal expenses at home, will you have the skills necessary to operate a million or multi-million dollar investment business? If you have filed bankruptcy before, take time to make some serious financial changes in your life. Otherwise, you run the risk of being left with liens on your properties and many foreclosures. For my game plan to work, it is essential for you to pay all bills and contractors promptly and establish a good reputation and credit rating.

The Myth of Get-Rich-Quick

I want to take a moment to warn you that there is no "instant wealth" in real estate, in spite of what you've heard on television. There can be, however, substantial monetary rewards which you work for and earn. Sometimes you can get lucky and make more than you usually do, but I can assure you, there is no deal where you can "instantly" make a fortune. So avoid these temptations as you invest.

The reality is that your first purchase will be a property with excellent cash flow. (Most investors who take the time to study the market manage to do all right the first time.) This will build not only self-confidence but also the desire to obtain another. From there, the need to purchase more can build up like an addiction. When a great bargain is found, the temptation to purchase will be so unbearable that you will do just about anything to close the deal. There is always the fear that this new deal will be impossible to top. If you've run out of available cash, you borrow off of an existing investment to purchase the new one. So begins your downfall.

To avoid these setbacks, you'll need to seek other ways to acquire cash to buy more real estate. I suggest that you refer to Chapter 5, which covers sources of investment funds, and Chapter 12, which shows how to take advantage of opportunities to resell for quick profits.

Part II
Researching
Investment Property

3

Choosing
Investment Property

With your primary investment goal fixed in your mind, it's time to consider the type of property that will give you the highest return on the money you'll invest. This chapter contains very specific guidelines as to the physical characteristics, location and profitability of prospective purchases. As I've mentioned earlier, the properties that have consistently given me the best return are not gilt-edged, high-rent homes in fashionable neighborhoods. While my investments are in areas that could be classified as low-income communities, they have certainly not afforded me a "low income"! In addition, I have had the personal satisfaction of knowing that the properties I own are well-maintained and are an asset to the surrounding neighborhood. Here is what I look for.

Type Of Units

I have found that three-bedroom-per-side doubles, bought right, offer the best opportunity for investment. These yield the highest return of any real estate available. Two-bedroom doubles are acceptable but yield a slight reduction in rent per unit for the same investment and labor, perhaps $25-$75 per month less. For this reason, when considering buying a two-bedroom per side double, be sure that it is an unusually good deal.

Stay away from two-storey, up-and-down duplexes. Resale and repair are problems on these. Generally, to work on the upstairs unit, you must bother the downstairs tenant. The side-by-side double is much easier to maintain for two reasons: you won't be troubling the next door neighbor and, more importantly, both sides have their own basement. The tenants enjoy their own storage and laundry facilities and you, as the landlord, have easy access for plumbing and heating repairs. From a management standpoint, you'll find that tenants are more apt to feud when one resides above the other. Side-by-side units structurally provide more privacy and separation for the tenants.

Single-family houses and brick row townhouses command higher purchase prices because of their supposed tenant selection and lower upkeep, but their return on investment is usually not as good. Since your goal is to achieve profit maximization with your initial investment program, single homes, townhouses, condominiums, and apartment complexes are out of the question until you have acquired and completed twenty functional doubles, even if they are not fully paid off. Only then, when the doubles have provided you with a strong financial base, should you begin to consider other types of investments.

Now that my business is well-established, I vary my purchases, while still relying on those profitable three-bedroom-per-side doubles for the bulk of my portfolio. Occasionally I see bargains that I simply can't pass up. Recently, for example, I've seen two decent single houses each selling for $2,500 and less. Investments like these would be ideal for restoration and resale, and would provide cash for additional purchases.

As another example, I bought a ten-unit apartment building for $60,000 (a bargain not found in every market, of course). With my $20,000 down payment the balance of $40,000 was financed by the seller for eight years. After many repairs and rental increases, the rents have exceeded $30,000 per year. But it's important to remember that it's wise to concentrate on three-bedroom-per-side doubles. This is where you get the most for your money.

Novices or those with low investment dollars should start slowly and should buy doubles that are currently occupied. This generally indicates a functional level of condition for the electrical, heating and plumbing systems. Tenants can answer questions about any past and current problems. Boarded-up buildings require someone who is experienced at rehabilitation.

Adjusting to Different Markets

While three-bedroom-per-side doubles are widely available throughout the United States, you may find that in your city, there may be no such properties from which to choose. Housing styles and real estate markets do vary. However, there is bound to be one particular type of unit that will meet all of the other guidelines in this book, including location and profit potential. It will take research on your part to determine which investment best follows the strategy I have outlined.

Why Doubles?

When I began investing, I focused entirely on single family dwellings. Like many other small investors, I calculated that if I at least broke even or had a small cash flow on a million dollars worth of real estate, I would someday become a millionaire. It sounded logical and I went ahead with my plan. After I had bought two houses, while working full-time to support my family, my father began to take an interest in my exploits and researched other possibilities for me. His early criticism had, by then, evolved into encouragement. Soon he advised me to buy doubles, rather than singles and his argument was quite simple and brief: both singles and doubles each have one roof, but with the double, you can collect two rents. In other words, the external repairs on each are virtually the same. For two rents, I need to maintain only one building, rather than two. Furthermore, it occurred to me that I might even make some money right away with two rent checks arriving.

Less than a month later, I closed on my first double, eager to see how it would work out. It was amazing! On rent day, I went to one building and collected two rents. The first rent paid all of the bills; the other was all cash flow. This one double did better than my two singles put together. Moreover, I soon discovered that a double was, and is, in most cases comparatively cheaper in price than a single, and owners of doubles were more willing to finance them. That was all it took to convince me to buy more doubles. Not only was my goal of becoming a millionaire realistic now, but I could also earn a monthly income while I was paying off the loans.

Location: Choose Only One Area

As you acquire rental properties, you will soon realize how important it is to have all units within close proximity of one another, so plan to confine all of your purchases to one neighborhood. The repairs or rehabilitation of the units, ongoing maintenance, and rent collections will all be far more convenient. In addition, the time and gasoline you'll save will be considerable. If you accumulate buildings all over the city, it becomes a burden to maintain them.

When I buy rental property, I do so with the intention of keeping the units. So I take particular care to choose investments that I will be happy with over the long term. Investors who are late in discovering the importance of close proximity end up selling and trading solely for the purpose of consolidating their properties. Not only are closing costs expensive, but at resale, there are taxes to pay on capital gains. So avoid the additional expense and hassle by choosing just one neighborhood for investment.

The Choice of Neighborhood

Select an older inner-city neighborhood where you feel comfortable working. Remember that your master plan is to keep everything that you buy, so spend ample time investigating your prospective investment area. Make sure that there is an adequate supply of properties from which to choose; I look for run-down and boarded-up buildings, since these can be sure signs of great buys in the neighborhood. However, do not choose the worst neighborhood in the city—and let me emphasize this. In the roughest of areas, rents will be considerably lower and tenant problems will be greater.

So research the neighborhood carefully. Since I have found that my best investments have been in decent low-income areas, I suggest that you look for just such a neighborhood, preferably one which has a very long, high-traffic thoroughfare. Confine all your purchases to that busy street and to property which you can actually see from there. This high visibility generally reduces litter, vandalism, break-ins, and drug-dealing. Later after you have acquired some property in the area, you will learn exactly which side streets, although distant from the thoroughfare, are good for investment.

Profit Projection

Property selection is the foundation of your game plan, since it ultimately dictates your cash flow. The neighborhood choice, type of rental units, cost of upkeep and debt amount all play an integral role in achieving maximum income and success.

Using as an example doubles which I own in Columbus, Ohio, an investor could receive two different market rents for two identical units within one neighborhood. Consider the busy thoroughfare we discussed earlier. Even in the closely-defined area in which you've decided to buy, there will be a "less desirable section" and an "upscale section". Although both are in the same general neighborhood, the rents differ. In the less-desirable section of my own investment area, one can rent a three-bedroom-per-side double for $325-$350 per month. In the upscale section, this same unit will rent for $375-$400 per side. Don't restrict your purchases to just the upscale section. Give yourself more opportunity for property acquisition by buying properties in both parts of the neighborhood. You may even find that your improvements will eventually upgrade the less-desirable section.

At times, there may be another kind of rent charged for units of this type, rent which is higher than my two examples above. This rent comes from your local Metropolitan Housing Authority, through a program called Section 8. You'll find details about this government assistance program in chapter 9.

In the calculations that follow, we'll use as our example the figures from six different properties I own, all of which are three-bedrooms-per-side doubles. Two of these (Group A) are in the less-desirable section of my investment neighborhood, two are in the upscale section (Group B) and two are Section 8 rentals (Group C). When projecting profits from our investment examples, we'll use the conservatively low rents from each group; in Group A, for instance, we'll use the figure of $650 per month for both units. The profit from these units depends on the debt amount, expenses, and vacancy rate. Since our aim is to have the properties paid for, we'll assume that there is no debt. Now let's try to calculate a realistic cash flow.

We'll start by establishing the true rental income. Beginning investors might assume that you just simply multiply $650 x 12. Bankers factor in repair and vacancy percentages to project income on purchases. However, I find it more accurate to use figures from my own Form 1040 federal income tax return. Below you will see a breakdown of income for each of the six different properties.

All of the tenants in the examples below are each billed monthly through a private meter reading service and pay their own water bills. These amounts are included in the rental income figures, as well as late and tenant-damage charges. For this reason, some of the annual income figures shown are higher than the actual rent charged.

The amounts listed below also include actual vacancies and nonpays based on my Form 1040.

Group A

Form 1040 Annual Income		Rents	Mo. Income
Property 1:	$ 7716.58	$ 325/$ 325	$ 643.05
Property 2:	$ 7662.08	$ 325/$ 325	$ 638.51

Now we must expense Properties 1 and 2 by using the actual figures from the tax forms.

Annual Expenses	Property 1	Property 2
Advertising	$ 29.90	$ 31.00
Insurance	$ 253.00	$ 258.00
Legal Fees	$ 105.00	
Repairs	$ 555.06	$ 983.02
Real Estate Taxes	$ 468.66	$ 390.98
Utilities (Water)	$ 693.54	$ 458.12
Total Expenses	$2105.16	$2121.12
Gross Monthly Income	$ 643.05	$ 638.51
Total Monthly Expense	$ 175.43	$ 176.76
Total Monthly Net	$ 467.62	$ 461.75
Total Yearly Net	$5611.44	$5541.00

Repair costs for the previous year reflect new carpets and paint. Remember that the monthly income figures include water charges, late fees, and vacancies.

Now let's move up to where the rents are a little higher and see what happens to sample properties in the upscale section of my investment area.

Group B

Form 1040 Annual Income	Rents	Mo. Income
Property 3: $8728.87	$ 355 / $ 375	$ 727.41
Property 4: $9303.63	$ 375 / $ 375	$ 775.30

Annual Expenses	Property 3	Property 4
Advertising	$ 19.00	$ 40.10
Insurance	$ 310.50	$ 262.00
Legal Fees	$ 125.00	$ 91.00
Repairs	$ 850.40	$ 193.10
Real Estate Taxes	$ 336.80	$ 465.84
Utilities	$ 363.02	$ 863.78
Total Expenses	$2004.72	$1915.82
Gross Monthly Income	$ 727.41	$ 775.30
Total Monthly Expense	$ 167.06	$ 159.65
Total Monthly Net	$ 560.35	$ 615.65
Total Yearly Net	$6724.20	$7387.80

Quite surprisingly, the doubles from the less-desirable section of the neighborhood fell short only $1000 in income per double per year. Had I not overhauled Properties 1 and 2, paying for extensive repairs, they might have come in a close second to Properties 3 and 4. Since I prefer to take a conservative approach by calculating the final figures on the low side, we'll use these numbers as they stand.

The examples in Group A and Group B demonstrate the two open markets at each end of my investment neighborhood. Now let's consider two similar properties in a different rental light. The Section 8 program pays a premium on the rental amount. However, it does expect a level of excellence from the Section 8 landlords.

Group C

Form 1040 Annual Income	Rents	Mo. Income
Property 5: $ 9735.80	$ 388 /$ 389	$ 811.32
Property 6: $ 9808.52	$ 395 /$ 410	$ 817.38

Annual Expenses	Property 5	Property 6
Advertising		
Insurance	$ 320.84	$ 232.00
Repairs	$ 492.61	$ 694.62

Real Estate Taxes	$ 438.54	$ 434.54
Utilities	$ 450.19	$ 742.68
Total Expenses	$1702.18	$2103.84
Total Monthly Income	$ 811.32	$ 817.32
Total Monthly Expense	$ 141.85	$ 175.32
Total Monthly Net	$ 669.47	$ 642.00
Total Yearly Net	$8033.64	$7704.00

As you can see, these units are bringing in a substantial income. The Section 8 program is an excellent way to improve cash flow, if you can tolerate and pass the inspections and reinspections required. When you have fewer than thirty units, it really is not too difficult to accommodate the Section 8 demands in order to acquire those higher rents. In addition, when you're starting to build your portfolio of investment properties, the higher return is especially welcome. However, once you have more than thirty units, you'll find that the time limitations imposed on Section 8 rentals often do not coincide with the deadlines that you have set for yourself on other projects. I suggest a variety of all three types of rentals as described above to make it easier on yourself. Include a mix of less-desirable and upscale area properties in your portfolio. Then periodically, add some Section 8 tenants as your time permits.

Briefly, let's itemize the three groups from above and make some conclusions.

Group A	Group B	Group C
$ 467.62	$ 560.35	$ 669.47
$ 461.75	$ 615.65	$ 642.00

To *income average*, total all six net incomes and divide by six. In the examples above, you'll find that the average monthly net income for these investment properties is $569.47. It would be unrealistic to base your averaging on only one type of rental— Group C, for instance. Be sure to run your calculations on the full range of properties, since this represents a true-to-life scenario. Perhaps you're surprised to see that there is such a wide variation in rents for similar units within the boundaries of one neighborhood. This diversity certainly adds flavor to your investments.

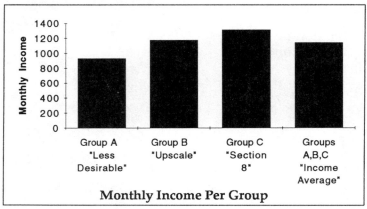

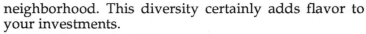

Monthly Income Per Group

As you recall, your goal will be to accumulate twenty doubles and eventually have them paid off. Based on prices in my investment area, with these projections I can comfortably estimate clearing a minimum of $550 per month per double. When multiplied by twenty, this equals a net income of $110,000 per year. With financing, these acquisitions are entirely possible to achieve within an eight- to fifteen-year time frame. By now you understand the reason my investment strategy places such heavy emphasis on cash flow. After all, income is the answer to your financial needs, and cash flow is the key to obtaining that income.

My Rule of Thumb for Buying Investment Property

*When acquiring or assuming financing, I must net $100 per unit, or $200 per double, after all monthly expenses, and I make every effort to pay off the debt in a short period of time. This rule of thumb is based not on **current rents** but rather on the rents I **expect** to charge. This is why I cannot purchase properties owned by the pseudo-investors, whose properties are heavily financed and whose goal is simply to break even. The margin of profit I require just isn't there.*

The Return on Your Investment: An Overview

For those who like to work with formulas and statistics, I will show you how to calculate the return on your investment. But first let's take a simplified view of the calculations involved. If, for example, you paid cash for twenty doubles and you averaged $20,000 on each, you would have paid a total of $400,000. If you net $569.47 per property like I did above, you would multiply this figure by twenty doubles, giving you a monthly cash flow of $11,389.40. Multiply by 12 to find the yearly cash flow of $136,672.80. Divide this figure by $400,000 (your total cash investment) and the return would be over 34 percent.

Annual Cash Flow / Amount Invested = Rate Of Return
     $136,672.80 / $400,000   =   .3417%

Purchase prices in your region may be twice those in my area. However, the same formula applies because your rents will also reflect a proportionate increase. Consider that both the cash flow and the amount invested are doubled for your area.

Annual Cash Flow / Amount Invested = Rate Of Return
     $273,335.60 / $800,000   =   .3417%

As I have illustrated, prices and rents are different throughout the country, but the rents will reflect purchase prices. There is no need to sacrifice the rate of return by paying higher prices elsewhere. The increased cash flow will provide full compensation for your investment plan You can achieve the same results. As the saying goes, "It's all relative." In my investment neighborhood here in Ohio, the doubles of the type I buy often are listed between $30,000 and $40,000. With careful shopping and negotiating, I buy similar doubles at around $20,000, with monthly incomes of approximately $700 per double. However, real estate prices in your area may be much higher. For example, average listing prices may be $50,000 to $60,000 on the type of property I would buy—and as a shrewd investor, you'd buy it for $40,000.

(In the following chapter I'll tell you how!) However, if your market prices are higher, your rents will be correspondingly high also. The dollar amounts are all relative for your respective region. The concept and strategy remains the same except for down payments involving larger commissions based on higher selling prices. Simply, insure that your projected return on each investment exceeds 20 percent.

Does Financing Affect Your Rate of Return?

Surprisingly, if you finance $14,000, with a $2,000 cash down payment, the return on your investment is a little higher. If your initial down payment and immediate repairs total $6,000 and you net $200 per month, take the yearly return of $2,400 and divide it by the investment amount. The return on investment is 40 percent. Even allowing for a 30 percent vacancy and maintenance allowance you will get a return of 28 percent. You could install Section 8 tenants in your units and, with the higher rents, get an even better return. Once I owned a double that yielded a 198 percent return, but that was an unusual situation. On the whole, it is much safer and wiser to expect a lower, more realistic return on your entire portfolio. Estimating a return of 34 percent is both conservative and attainable.

Don't Overlook Expenses

Do not create an illusion of wealth by estimating a cash flow and return on investment that fails to build in expenses and repair costs. This is how many investors are duped into paying higher prices for investment properties. They see the rents at $750 per month, with a monthly payment of $450, and visualize receiving $300 per month on this $40,000 property. But this $300 will never be realized. If you recheck the six monthly figures above, you will find that the monthly expenses alone range from $141 to $176. After subtracting $176, the investor will really receive a menial $124 per month. So begins the regret and the disenchantment with real estate investment.

The most absurd rule of thumb that I have ever heard is the one that calculates a property's worth by its monthly rental income. Here's how it goes: according to this theory, if the gross monthly rent collection is $700, then the property is worth $70,000. In other words, the premise that the property is worth 100 times the monthly gross rent. After you've worked through the calculations with me, as we determined the cash flow from the sample properties and established the rate of return on the investment, can you imagine anyone believing that ridiculous guideline? What happened to repair costs, miscellaneous expenses, and current market prices for comparable properties? You would be surprised at the number of buyers who swallow this theory whole, and you'd be astonished at the number of times I've heard it repeated. To support this theory, one "expert" claims that it really does not matter what a buyer pays, providing the rents support the purchase price. Unfortunately this is very bad advice, and I feel genuinely sorry for investors who have been taken in by it.

Calculating Your Rate of Return

Add the monthly mortgage payment, taxes and insurance to figure your PITI. Find 30 percent of the monthly gross rents to calculate a vacancy and maintenance allowance. Subtract the PITI and the 30 percent allowance from your monthly gross rents to find the conservative monthly cash flow amount. Multiply by 12 to find the annual cash flow. Include the down payment and initial projected repairs in the amount invested.

Annual Cash Flow/Amount Invested = Over 20% Rate of Return

This ultra-conservative calculation sets the framework for a successful project by providing a wide margin for error and miscalculation.

The worksheets on the following page will help you calculate your anticipated rate of return on potential investments or your actual rate of return on properties you currently own.

Calcul

Cash dc

Add ba
    (M(
      mo
Rent pr
Real es
Tenant
Earnes
Estima

Subtot

Subtra
    (C
Daily
Mortg

Total

Calculating a Conservative Cash Flow

Monthly principal and interest on all loans:	$_____
Monthly taxes and insurance:	±_____
Monthly PITI:	$_____
Monthly rents:	$_____
Monthly PITI:	−_____
30 percent of monthly rents:	−_____
(Vacancy and maintenance allowance)	
Total monthly cash flow:	$_____
	x 12
Total annual cash flow:	$_____

Rate of Return Formula:

Annual Cash Flow / Amount Invested = Rate of Return

4

How To Locate Great Buys

E ach deal I close seems to be even better than the last. As I complete one transaction, it makes me wonder if I'll ever be as lucky in the future. But I always come through with another. In fact, people invariably ask how I manage to find such deals. They can't imagine that they have access to the same resources as I, to locate and purchase these great buys.

At a glance, it may seem that there are no real estate bargains available in your city. If I were to open a Multiple Listing Service book, for example, I'd see the cheapest double in my investment neighborhood to be listed at about 150% of the price I usually pay. But armed with a little information about where and how to look, and the patience to wait for those great buys, I can sleuth out exceptional deals and you can too, no matter what the real estate market is like in your area.

Of course most sellers want a buyer to come close to their asking price. This does not, however, mean that they will not sell at a cheaper price if the conditions are right for a quick sale. About two years ago, I bought two doubles across the street from each other, with the closings on the same day. They were owned by different sellers and listed with different real estate agents. The asking price on each was $29,900. The selling price on each was, coincidently, $20,000. Why did the sellers both accept such low offers? Very simple: both sellers had difficulties with their tenants, both sellers owned just one piece of rental property and both buildings needed exterior paint. The sellers were motivated to sell immediately, and competition from other buyers was greatly reduced because the buildings were unattractive and needed work. This is the ideal situation. If you can track down a property with no curb appeal, an eager seller and an absence of prospective buyers, you'll very likely benefit from the circumstances.

It is up to you, the buyer, to gather as much information about the property and its owner that the seller's real estate agent is permitted to divulge. Usually the seller will authorize this information to be told to prospective buyers because he wants a quick sale and also because he is required to do so. Known repair problems and code violations must be divulged before the contract, but be wary of misrepresentation. In your initial contact with the sales agent, ask questions that will yield information about the seller's motivation and financial status.

Often one call to the selling agent will squelch any possibility of a deal. You'll discover that the mortgage balance is too high or the seller thinks that his building is laced with 22-karat gold. If the selling agent states, "He doesn't have to sell it," end the conversation right there. Obviously the seller has no motivation. I have never bought a property from someone who told me this; it should be a tip-off that this deal is not right for you either. Keep looking for a better prospect.

Sources for the Best Buys

1. Real Estate Agents

Some properties are listed with real estate agents, although they are not in the M.L.S. book. These are generally found with a sign in the yard and through local advertising. This may be a new listing or a property listed by an agent or broker not affiliated with the Multiple Listing Service. So be alert for For Sale signs in your investment area and inquire about the property immediately. Once you've made contact with an agent, leave detailed information about the type of property you're interested in, for the agent's future reference. Conscientious agents are quick to notify serious investors as soon as a likely property is listed.

Eventually, you may want to acquire a real estate license yourself. As a licensee, you'll represent yourself and earn a commission on the sale. Information about a property can be obtained quickly, without relying on an agent to ferret it out and call back. You will have access to the local Multiple Listings Service, with its books and computer listings of properties for sale. A license will give you closer contact with sellers and will allow you to ask questions directly.

You may want to accumulate a number of properties before obtaining a real estate license, to see if this is the career for you, since the exams require considerable study and there are additional expenses associated with that license. Until you acquire your real estate license, find a competent agent to work with.

2. Newspaper Advertisements

Subscribe to the Sunday edition of the largest newspaper in your city. You'll be using this resource later to advertise your rental vacancies, but when you're looking for investment property, the Sunday real estate or investment section classifieds provide an excellent listing of properties available for sale by the owners themselves. There may be a section called "Investment Property Residential" or perhaps "Duplexes, Etc." In it you'll find small ads stating the address, price, and the willingness of the seller to finance. Here's a tip: A fast way to scan all the classified ads is to look for the smallest real estate ad. Pay special attention to ads with these phrases: "Out of state owner," "Must sell," and "Owner finance." Skip over titles which read "Quality investment property," "New," or "Remodeled." Remember, if you're looking for a great buy, you want "desperate" and "dilapidated".

Check the Sunday paper early because not only do you want to have the first showing, but you want to reach the seller before the real estate agents do. They "work" the paper just like you, except they want listings. Once the property is listed, it will cost more to buy and the owner will need sufficient cash (usually out of the down payment) to pay the commission. So be there first and buy at a lower price and with a smaller down payment.

3. Legal Newspapers

In a large city, you'll find a newspaper that deals primarily with legal documentation. All lawsuits, vendors' licenses, new corporations, bankruptcies, and other legal notices are listed there. The one item in particular that attracts my attention is the list of foreclosures. In my local legal paper, the foreclosures are listed in Tuesday's edition only. While some newspapers permit you to order the paper for one particular day of the week only, mine requires a full subscription. So I pay my $75.00 for the entire year's home delivery, examine Tuesday's edition for the foreclosures and recycle the others after reading just the front page.

Our legal newspaper lists pages and pages of current foreclosures, each listed for five weeks. If you have already selected your prospective neighborhood and are familiar with the streets, you can scan this paper in just a few minutes. Search for an item that shows two different house numbers. This indicates a double. Then read further to find the appraised value. If it is very low, you're in business. Now check the auction date, and give the property a drive-by inspection. If the conditions are right, get your money ready. You'll need to bring a cashier's check to the auction, usually 10% of the appraisal price, so be sure to check the local requirements and amount necessary for this particular property.

The balance is due within 30 days. However, conditions of the sale may be different for your area. If you're purchasing property this way, make certain that the price is dirt cheap because you'll usually be buying with no interior inspection of the premises. I find that the windows are often boarded up, so visual inspection is very difficult.

4. Boarded-up Properties

As I've recommended in Chapter 3, confine your purchases, at first, to habitable doubles until you've developed an expertise at estimating property values and repair costs, and have acquired the necessary labor pool. But once you've reached this level of expertise, boarded-up properties can be exceptionally profitable investments.

Often you'll spot a run-down building that you feel could be a good buy. To find the owner, just call the county map room for the district and parcel number. Then call the county tax room, and they will give you the address to which the tax bills are mailed. With the address in hand, try matching the owner's name to one in the telephone book. This works occasionally. If the phone number is unlisted, try writing a letter. If a mortgage company is listed for tax mailings, it will be difficult or impossible to get information.

An easier method to acquire property information is to call a title insurance company that offers a *lien check* service. For a small fee, they will uncover the property and mortgage information. Real estate agents who regularly close deals there are offered the same service, often under a different name, such as a *realty assist*.

5. Properties Near Yours

There have been many occasions when I have bought the building next door to or near one I already own. I make a point of talking to my new tenants and to the tenants next door. Sometimes I offer a finder's fee if I purchase the property that they tell me about. Once you own your first rental, you'll now have an opportunity to talk to the landlords of other properties in the immediate vicinity. They may have that property and others to sell as well.

Keep an eye out for "apartment-for-rent" signs; it never hurts to jot down the number, call the owner and ask if he wants to sell.

6. Other Contacts

Other good sources for leads are all the people you talk to about real estate. It's so easy to leave your name and phone number with anyone who might hear about a property you'd be interested in. Ask them to give you a call if something comes up even six months later. Many agents keep my name on file now and call me as soon as they list a property, before it has even reached the M.L.S. book. Keep in contact with other investors. If they decide to sell, perhaps they'll remember to call you first. When you close a transaction, let the seller, both real estate agents and anyone else at the closing table know that you're interested in hearing about other properties that are available now or in the future.

Once your business is well established, a few properties will simply drop in your lap. It's strange: you'll wear yourself out searching for another property to buy and someone will call out of the clear blue with a great deal. This is, of course, not the most reliable source of investment property, but it does help you pick up an additional rental now and then.

7. Associations

If you have a real estate license, there are often breakfast meetings and seminars for groups of agents. Find a group that meets regularly and get to know other agents and investors. The key here is to locate and attend the meetings in and near the neighborhood you have targeted for your investment. Real estate agents who work that area are excellent contacts.

There are real estate investment clubs where every investor (and would-be investor) is welcome to join. Their meetings are usually posted in the investment section of the Sunday newspaper. At these meetings, a special time is set aside for investors to get together and exchange information. It's a great opportunity to buy, sell, trade, or make excellent contacts.

What Motivates Sellers?

In the type of investment property I recommend— what might be characterized as "low-income housing"— you will find plenty of desperate sellers who can't wait to get out of the real estate business. This may be due either to the sellers' absolute frustration in dealing with troublesome tenants or to financial troubles resulting from bad investment decisions.

Although later in this book I'll cover the subject of management difficulties thoroughly, it helps to understand the problems most likely to cause investors to bail out. First, let's evaluate how troublesome tenants can produce a willing seller.

The Motivating Force of Tenant Problems

The problems usually begin when a tenant fails to pay rent. Often tenants themselves or the Children's Services Division will call the city code enforcement to report code violations. Many tenants, through ignorance of the law, believe that if the unit is in need of repair, there is just cause not to pay rent (although be aware that tenants' rights laws vary from state to state). In reality, here is what often happens after such a call: the tenant is evicted and the landlord is given a deadline by the code inspector to complete the repairs. A nonpaying tenant who should be evicted gives a seller motivation to sell quickly. City code violations with deadlines to be met will give the seller additional impetus to unload the property as soon as possible.

Case History: Tenant problems? Slumlord problems!

I recently purchased a double from a seller who had owned the building for thirty-one years. His problem began when a Children Services official visited the unit and notified the Code Enforcement Division about the deplorable condition of the interior and exterior of the building. The landlord was from the "old school" tradition: he collected rents and made no repairs. To put it bluntly, he was a slumlord. You can imagine the horrendous condition of the building, after thirty-one years of serious neglect. Needless to say, the city inspector listed three pages of violations on the one unit alone. Actually, considering the appalling condition of the property, I'm amazed that this man lasted as long as he did without experiencing the wrath of a city inspector.

I came along and offered to purchase his property when the repairs were nearly completed. I had learned, through another landlord, of his desire to sell. Fortunately for me, he had just put on a new roof and two coats of exterior paint. There was a tenant on one side and the other side was vacant. Since the vacant side had not yet been inspected by the city, I am sure that the owner was worried about the results of such an inspection. He was deliberately not renting the vacant side for fear of further exposure to the relentless city inspector.

For him, this double, which had once generated two rents with very minimal expenses, suddenly turned into a one-rent investment with astronomical repairs. This made the situation ideal for me. When I came along, all of the extensive and expensive exterior repairs had been completed and one of the units had been slightly overhauled. Needless to say, I caught him at the right moment.

The seller owned the double free and clear, so he was able to walk away from the closing table with over $17,000 of the $18,000 sales price. While the money was no doubt welcome, the sale meant the end of a living nightmare for him. So why would I want it?

When I ran my calculations (as we did in the previous chapter), I discovered that the property could indeed be a money-maker.

Today, all of the repairs have been made, and I sure look forward to finding another deal like this one. I rehabilitated the vacant unit and moved the present tenant to the unit next door, raising the rent from $300 to $325. She was eager to cooperate. Her family had never enjoyed brand new carpet before. Then I completed the work the previous owner had started on the once-occupied unit, which I then rented for $350. It was that simple. Would I rather have my $18,000 and repair money back, and give up $675 per month in rent? Not at all! But obviously, the seller would. I have found that so often the wrong attitude, coupled with ignorance, can drastically hinder an investor's performance and lead to certain failure.

Code Violations Push Owners to Sell

Owners who are faced with nonpaying tenants and code violation repairs often suffer from a high level of frustration, especially if they own just one to three properties and have a full-time career as well. Citation for code violations are serious; in many communities, a landlord risks a jail term for noncompliance if repairs are not made within the allotted deadline. So a code violation is excellent motivation for a frustrated owner to reduce the price and dump the property, instead of pouring more repair money into it. Once the deed is transferred, all of the seller's code enforcement problems end. There are plenty of investors who, rather than paint the exterior of the unit, would sell it for a fraction of its value. This is the ideal situation for serious buyers. Almost every purchase I make is from this category of sellers and I suggest that this particular category should be your primary target. When you locate a building where these conditions apply, negotiate a great deal immediately. Strike while the iron is hot. Before you agree to purchase any property, always ask if there are written code violations and request to see the list. Watch out for sellers who have no intention of informing you of them, unless you specifically ask.

Financial Problems Motivate Sellers

Sellers sometimes find themselves in financial situations which force them to try to liquidate their assets immediately. As a rule, these are not the properties that you'll want to purchase. As I emphasized in chapter two, the main cause of financial difficulty for investors is poor cash flow. If the seller paid too much for the property originally and is financially buried in it, then it's not a good buy. The debt against the property will prevent the owner from lowering the sales price to a reasonable level. However, it's a good idea to make contact anyway, to ask the owner if he or she has any other properties available. You could find a hidden deal that way.

Boarded-up Bargains Abound

Boarded-up buildings could be a result of the problems I've just discussed. A bank may have repossessed the double and boarded it up. Or perhaps the current landlord boarded it up himself because he was frustrated with bad tenants or was afraid of city code violations. If the city code enforcement agency condemned the building and the landlord did not make the required repairs, the city may have stepped in and boarded-up the units.

Consider Estate Sales

You may be fortunate to find a bargain property in an estate sale, although they are hard to come by. When an owner dies, the heirs often want to cash out quickly, but usually there is one heir who is a bit greedy and wants more than you want to spend. However, there are some bargains to be found. For example, I'll be closing a deal shortly which involves five heirs. The purchase price for the now-vacant three-bedroom-per-side double is $10,500. The heirs fear further vandalism and theft, so they are anxious to sell. This is only one of a very few which I have bought from an estate.

Negotiate the Best Deal for Yourself

Don't feel guilty for taking advantage of someone else's problems. After all, the sellers do have the option of evicting the tenants and making the repairs themselves. In reality, most sellers in this situation are thrilled to dump the city violations and nonpaying tenants in your lap and to leave the closing table laughing at the buyer who is naive enough (in the sellers' opinion) to pay money for a parcel of problems. So negotiate the best deal that you can for yourself. The sellers are under no obligation to sign the contract if they don't want to. Besides, at the closing table, the title insurance agent will ask the sellers if they are signing over the deed with "sound mind and free will". My sellers have always said yes, and more often than not, they laugh in my face at the closing. I don't let that bother me. My success with these properties gives me the last laugh.

You May Have the Field to Yourself

People invest in real estate for many different reasons. My strategy is directed toward investment as a means of attaining financial independence. It's important to me to purchase properties that will generate the cash flow to allow me to reach my goal. Other investors buy rentals as write-offs or future retirement nest eggs, while they continue to work at full-time jobs. They don't want to be bothered by their investments and they choose rentals that will not require much upkeep and maintenance. A management company can be employed to collect the rents and to facilitate repairs. Many of them would be embarrassed if friends considered them a slumlord. They want to own property that is impressive to show off. More expensive rentals are perfect for these investors whose primary goal is to break even. If the property they buy meets their particular investment criteria, fine. It would certainly not lead me closer to my goal.

Of the relatively few investors who do invest in low-income neighborhoods, most set strict guidelines as to which properties they will buy. They hope to limit their expenses and headaches by not purchasing units that need painting or have city code violations. But the joke is on them; this is exactly what contributes most to their failure. They want the cash flow without the work. They want to acquire the nicer property in the low-income neighborhood and to earn a magnificent cash flow. This is pseudo-investing. Moreover, it is impossible to accomplish. These investors initially pay too much for the units and eventually become financially buried in them. Along the way, they'll find that they've acquired the same tenant problems and repair expenses that they would have incurred by buying the less-attractive property, but their return on investment is far lower than it could have been. If they are not willing to take on properties that require hands-on attention and constant nurturing, then these pseudo-investors should stick to the beautiful properties in upscale neighborhoods, pay the higher prices, and strive to break even.

Most of us cannot afford to just break even. There is too much work to do without adequate compensation. (If you take time here to reread my rule of thumb in chapter 3, you'll see why I cannot purchase properties owned by these pseudo-investors, since there is simply not the margin of profit I need.)

Because of the diversity of goals and strategies in real estate investment, you may be pleasantly surprised to find that competition is not as keen as you anticipated. The properties that yield the best returns are located in neighborhoods many pseudo-investors surprisingly enough avoid. So, although you'll have to be alert to bargains when they appear, you may have few prospective buyers actually bidding against you. And in bad economic times, the competition may practically disappear, leaving you a field of increasingly desperate sellers all to yourself.

Other Points to Consider

As you're looking for possible investment properties, you must always focus on **price** and **location**. As you know, "location" to many investors means finding a nice, upscale neighborhood, but not to me. Although equity position is important to me, increasing property values are never my prime consideration. In order to achieve profit maximization, I make sure that each and every purchase has an unbeatable price, and, if financed, has superb financing. Obviously, anything less would mean a lower profit schedule.

Personally, I prefer to buy doubles that are boarded up or in dire need of repair. They cost less initially and leave me with a larger cash allowance for repairs. When the renovation is complete, there is less money invested in my project and yet I now own a building where all the mechanical systems are new. In fact, if I need money, I could sell it and make at least $10,000 upon completion.

Be careful, though, that you do not own more than two boarded-up buildings at any one time. I know many investors who are buried in mortgage payments with no income from the unoccupied units to support the mortgage, not to mention the repairs. Then too, if money is not a consideration, vandalism and theft should be. If you're already working on two badly damaged buildings and a third deal tempts you, try stalling the contract or extending the closing date to accommodate your rehabilitation schedule.

A few years ago, I bought a double that was truly a pigsty for $13,000. The rents were $125 and $175. I spent another $5,500 on repairs. A couple of years later, I sold it for $32,500. After typical closing and agent expenses, I received a check for $30,072.02 at the closing. Clearly, I was not financially buried in the property like some of the other investors I've described. And this example points out one of the ways to acquire additional money to buy other properties: buy, fix, rent, and then sell. Do not— and I emphasize this— refinance to get reinvestment cash and get buried in the property, while working for free. Instead, profit from the sale and reinvest all the cash to achieve your goal of owning twenty doubles, free and clear. Granted, your goal is to acquire properties with the full intention of keeping them, but there are times when it is advantageous to resell for a profit to purchase more doubles. In this case, if my double had not sold, it would not have been a problem since it was in my selected neighborhood and had a tremendous cash flow. For a keepsake, I made a copy of the check, as a small reminder that every little deal has great potential.

Keep Track of Possible Buys

Use a thick notebook to consolidate all of the information you accumulate on potential real estate investments. Not only does it keep all the facts at your fingertips, but it makes it easier to contact the various sellers at a later date. Organization is important and this is much more efficient than having dozens of different messages and notations on pieces of paper.

My notebook has saved me plenty of money as well as frustration. I make a point of noting down information that sellers and their agents give me when I am considering a purchase. When the information is on paper it is very easy to stop back at the building to verify the facts that you were given. I don't trust sellers, as a rule. They are often desperate to unload their properties. So be extremely careful about what you sign. The most common trick will be to cheat you out of the tenant deposits which are rightfully yours when you purchase. I've often heard sellers state that the tenant owes them money, or that there are no deposits. Dishonest sellers have even signed affidavits to that effect. But with your notebook in hand, you can politely confront them about apparent discrepancies before you sign the closing documents. Chances are that they will back down and mumble that they will "let you have your way to close the deal."

When I was working in sales, I soon learned that I had to encounter many "nos" before a sale was made— a numbers game. Real estate is certainly no different. If you keep in mind that most of your inquiries will go nowhere and most offers will be rejected, then you will develop the patience and stamina to endure rejection until an offer is finally accepted.

The following chapter will take you a step closer to your goal, as we look at the various money sources and financing methods open to you.

Pre-Purchase Checklist

Estimate the major repairs needed before you negotiate. Check applicable boxes, and circle the option that describes the problem:

EXTERIOR

- ☐ Frayed or missing shingles; roof, tear-off, patch?
- ☐ Rotted soffit & fascia boards; 1,2,3, or 4 sides?
- ☐ Sagging or missing gutters; approx. ft. replacement?
- ☐ Crushed or missing downspouts; approx. ft. replacement?
- ☐ Major front or rear porch repair?
- ☐ Paint; trim or entire?
- ☐ Doors needed; how many?
- ☐ Electric meter box missing; how many?
- ☐ Water or gas line leaking in yard?
- ☐ Tree removal; how many?
- ☐ Tear down garage; 1 or 2 car?

INTERIOR

Basement

- ☐ Cracked or caving-in of walls; small or large area?
- ☐ Electric fuse or circuit breaker box missing; how many?
- ☐ Under 100 amp. service; how many?
- ☐ Missing furnace; how many?
- ☐ Ductwork; partial or entire?
- ☐ Inoperable furnace; how many?
- ☐ Hot water tank; how many?

Kitchen

- ☐ Cabinets w/sink; how many?
- ☐ Floor; how many?

Bathroom

- ☐ Toilet, sink, or bathtub; how many?
- ☐ Floor; how many?

General

- ☐ Paint; half, entire?
- ☐ Window replacement; how many?
- ☐ Light fixtures; how many?
- ☐ New Carpet; estimated sq. yds.?

Part III
Acquiring
Properties

5

Financing Your Investment Properties

Y ou'll need to have all of your financing methods down pat before your first offer to purchase is written. In this chapter I will outline several methods of purchasing (and paying for) real estate investments. Once you know the basics, you can tailor them to suit your personal financial capabilities.

Familiarize yourself with the amortization chart you'll find in the Appendix at the end of this book. It will enable you to sit at home and calculate payment schedules for the properties you wish to buy.

Cash for the Down Payment

In most cases, your cash down payment must be sufficiently large to cover the closing expenses of the sale, with enough left over to allow the seller to pocket a little cash. For my doubles, most of which are around $20,000 in price, I estimate $385 to $1,200 for the selling expenses alone. Real estate sales commissions and title insurance are the two main expenses. If you are investing in a city with a real estate market that is considerably higher priced than that of Columbus, Ohio, where I live, you'll have to allow a proportionately larger cash reserve.

Money Sources

No matter how much money you have, it seems that you always need more. Investing can be addictive: you're sure that if you just buy this one great bargain, you'll be happy. But as soon as that transaction is closed, another fantastic deal comes along. Now you need more money. Once you've successfuly completed a few great invest-ments, the thrill to purchase others will constantly nag at you to continue the search for more. More often than not, the need for additional capital will arise. So here are some tips for obtaining added funds.

Profitable Partnerships

After you have achieved a bit of a successful track record, friends and relatives will flock around you to see if there is any room for them. People love a success story, and it makes them feel as though they are missing the action, unless they can share a part of your adventure.

Years ago, after I had purchased enough properties to support my family, I quit my job very suddenly. I didn't ask for a reference, since by then I knew I'd never need or want another job. My father had occasionally taken the time to teach me to do some repair work and by then he acknowledged that I had finally overcome my reputation as a thread-stripper. Upon hearing that I quit my job and could support my family on my real estate alone, he pressured me to invest with him as well. This was good news because I needed money for acquisitions. Now he wanted to be my partner. He had evolved from critic to partner in a very short time. My father and I went on to purchase fourteen units together and I'm certain that if he had lived longer, we would have built up quite a successful partnership.

Be sure that with any partnership in which you partici-pate, you are completely in charge and make all the decisions. When possible, have your partner give you a limited power-of-attorney on each property, certifying that all decisions and responsibilities are yours. You may be able to find an investor willing to front all of the money in exchange for your expertise, management, and labor. Or you and your partner might work out a different arrangement: for instance, if the double is boarded up, your partner's contribution for the down payment and initial rehabilitation expenses could be three-fourths of the total and yours might be the remaining one-fourth. Or perhaps, if both units are occupied, the split could be two-thirds and one-third, with the financial input including both purchase costs and immediate repairs.

This same arrangement can and should apply to both cash deals and financed properties. Divide all rents equally from the day of purchase. To offset your partner's three-fourths or two-thirds investments, your contribution will be to work without pay on repairs, rent collection, evictions, and all other aspects of the investment business. When the property is sold, each partner receives his or her respective down payment and rehabilitation expenditures before the fifty-fifty split on profit. You benefit because you would not have that investment or profit without your partner's contribution. However, you'll work hard for your benefit.

It is vitally important that you communicate to your investment partner exactly what your goals and strategies are. Be sure that he or she understands that you wish to make extensive initial repairs and always keep the property in good rental condition. Investors with differing goals do not make congenial partners. You want anyone who invests in your business to be happy with the investment. After all, if you need further cash assistance, this partner would be the first place to seek it.

Building Your Cash Reserve

As I mentioned earlier, you may wish, on occasion, to buy a very inexpensive property and fix it up with the full intention of reselling it. This is an excellent way to build up a large cash reserve. Remember, this cash reserve is not your primary goal nor the means to attain it. Income is what you must focus your attention on. Once you have established a cash reserve from buying and selling or have acquired financing from another investor, you are well on your way. In Chapter 12, you will find a detailed explanation on how to fully execute this technique of buying for reselling.

Home-Equity Loans

Home-equity loans are certainly a way to obtain fast money, but I really do not favor this method at all. You'll be much better off working hard on your job while you try to save your overtime pay. At the same time, cut expenditures at home and consider trying to liquidate some expensive valuables like jewelry or sports cars. I know two investors whose fully paid-for Corvettes financed their initial ventures into rental real estate.

Try to avoid tapping into your home equity with a second mortgage. That has to be repaid, with monthly payments that can easily sabotage your investment efforts. While I do not adamantly oppose this technique, it certainly makes me feel uncomfortable when I see novice investors trying to get started this way. As you've probably concluded, I simply do not like borrowing money for down payments, entire purchases, or repairs.

Buying Methods

So far I've discussed ways to acquire seed money for down payments and closing costs. There are many different methods to finance the balance of the purchase. Be advised that state laws pertaining to purchase money mortgages and land contracts differ from state to state, so beginning investors should consult an attorney for advice. Here are some suggestions to consider, along with my comments and recommendations.

1. Simple VA and FHA Loan Assumptions

All VA (Veterans Administration) and FHA (Federal Housing Administration) loans are assumable, however in recent years some restrictions have been added. VA loans made prior to March 1, 1988 may be assumed without any need for the buyer to qualify. (Assumptions where qualifying is not mandatory are known as *simple assumptions* and are very desirable for investors.) VA loans originating after March 1, 1988 may be assumed only if the buyer makes formal application, qualifies for the loan and gives the seller a release of liability.

Old FHA loans, those originating prior to December 1986, may be assumed without qualifying. On FHA loans made to investors after December 1, 1986 and prior to December 15, 1989, the only restriction is that they must have been held for at least two years before they can be assumed via simple assumption. FHA loans made since December 15, 1989 are assumable by investors only if they are investor-originated 203ks. On these, the buyer must qualify for the assumption and give the seller a release of liability.

Simple assumptions are especially attractive to investors. Many of your buys will be financed by assuming existing loans. If the loan balance is fairly high compared to the purchase price, you can often assume these loans by just covering the selling costs. Of course these expenses may, at times, include a real estate commission on the sale, which increases the size of the required down payment.

Other times you must be more creative because the balance may be too low for an assumption alone. Here are different examples that involve VA and FHA loan assumptions. Be careful that you pay attention to both the purchase price and the interest rate— not just the down payment. Always remember that your goal is to pay off all of the debt on your doubles in the shortest period of time and with the lowest payment possible. Concentrate on maximum cash flow. If you do, your investments will earn a lot of money for you now and even more later.

Example A

This is a very simple deal: you assume the first mortgage balance and make the payments for the term of the loan. Incidentally, the property taxes and insurance are always included in the monthly payment on VA and FHA loans.

Price	$20,000	
Balance	$18,000	(Assume first mortgage)
Commissions and Expenses	$ 2,000	(Down payment)

Now, let's make a small but significant change.

Example B

In this case, with a smaller first mortgage loan, you will need an additional $8,000 to make the deal work— although not necessarily in cash. Your offer to purchase will now include provisions for the seller to hold a second mortgage for a total of $8,000 and you will make payments directly to him. Usually, on small amounts like this I suggest that the mortgage not exceed eight years.

Price	$20,000	
Balance	$10,000	(Assume first mortgage)
Commissions and Expenses	$ 2,000	(Down payment)
Need for Down payment	$ 8,000	(New 2nd mortgage)

You will have two payments to make on this double, one payment on each of the two mortgages. When the second mortgage is paid off, the cash flow automatically increases by the amount of the payment on the second, and you are well on your way to owning this property free and clear.

Example C

Your geographical location may result in prices that are twice the $20,000 that I pay. If so, these figures illustrate your situation. Your rate of return will be slightly lower than that in Examples A and B, based on the higher down payment.

Price	$40,000	
Balance	$37,000	(Assume first mortgage)
Commissions and Expenses	$ 3,000	(Down payment)

Price	$40,000	
Balance	$20,000	(Assume first mortgage)
Commissions and Expenses	$ 3,000	(Down payment)
Need for Down payment	$17,000	(New second mortgage)

When I consider making an offer on a property, I find that there is often $6,000 to $8,000 difference between the asking price and the loan balance. Here is your opportunity to negotiate a lower sales price. One good tactic is to tell the real estate agent that you can only permit yourself to spend just enough money to cover the expenses of the sale. Then indicate that you don't want a second mortgage because you must keep your expenses down. Often by using this tactic, you can shave off thousands of dollars; $2,500 to $3,000 in cash will often result in a deal for me.

To make this work, the seller must be very motivated to sell and must be convinced that there is no additional money to squeeze out of you. It is a game, of course, but ultimately you, the buyer, will win. If the seller does not sign the offer, buy something else and let him be stuck with his property. Incidentally, it never hurts to call back in thirty days and check the status— by then the seller may have regretted not accepting your offer.

This is, by far, my favorite way to purchase property. By lowering the sales price to a figure that allows an assumption and a low cash payment, you'll end up with a transaction that offers the cleanest, simplest and lowest-cost closing.

The assumption fee for a simple FHA or VA assumption is now $125, and the transaction is one that just about everyone understands. What I enjoy most is not going to the bank. For new loans and other types of assumptions, the bank lending fees and down payments are unappealing to me. When I started out, loan assumptions were my primary method to accumulate many properties because I had limited investment cash available to me.

Even if the interest rate on an FHA or VA loan seems high, it may still be worth assuming. A few lenders offer what is known as a Streamlined Refinance Without Appraisal. Once you've owned the property for six months, you may be eligible to refinance the assumed loan without an appraisal or credit report. Very few lenders offer this option, so to find one, contact the regional HUD (the federal Department of Housing & Urban Development, which manages the FHA loan program) or VA office (Department of Veterans Affairs) serving your community.

2. Purchase Money Mortgages (or Deeds of Trust)

When the target property has no loan on it, and you do not want to go to the bank for financing, let the seller finance it for you. One seller-financing method that I like very much is the *purchase money mortgage* (or *purchase money deed of trust*). It has an advantage over another commonly used financing vehicle, the land contract, (which I'll discuss next). With a purchase money mortgage, the buyer is given the deed to the property at closing. Here's how it works.

When you are writing the offer to buy, state the purchase price you want to pay, then specify the amount you're willing to pay as a cash down payment. Suggest that the seller take back a first mortgage and note for the entire balance due with an interest rate and term of your choosing. Specify an interest rate one to two points lower than the banks charge for their loans. (Remember, if you have chosen the property wisely, you have found a seller who is eager, if not desperate to sell.) Keep the term on the note as short as you can; personally, I like an eight year payout. This will, no doubt, eliminate all balloon payment ideas that the seller has in mind. (A *balloon payment* is a required early pay-off of the loan balance on a specific date.) Balloon payments are often very difficult to make when the time comes, and you put your ownership of the property in jeopardy by failing to make the pay-off when it is due. So avoid balloon payments and offer the seller a short-term note instead. You'll be taking some of the pain and plenty of the risk out of your investment.

Here is how a purchase money mortgage transaction might look:

Price $20,000.
Down payment $ 3,000.
Purchase $ Mtg. $17,000.   (8% For Eight Years)

With this method, you can be creative in specifying all the terms of this particular agreement, so work out an arrangement that suits your needs and one that the seller can find acceptable. You can also assume many existing purchase money mortgages, provided there is no clause in the documents forbidding an assumption. Just structure your assumption as you would a simple VA or FHA assumption.

Words of Good Advice

- Avoid new bank loans.
- Never buy with balloon payments.
- Selling with balloons is fine.

---

3. Land Contracts

A *land contract* (or *land sales contract*, or *contract for deed*, as it is often called) is another form of seller-financing agreement that may be used in place of the purchase money mortgage, when there is no existing loan. However, it can also be used when the seller has a loan already.

Some lenders will allow the seller and buyer to enter into a land contract agreement leaving the existing loan in place. The seller will make payments to the lender, while the buyer will make payments to the seller, based on the purchase price of the property. The problem with land contracts is that the deed is not transferred to the buyer at the time of purchase. For this reason, I am strongly opposed to this method of seller-financing.

When the lender does not permit a land contract, many buyers and sellers are tempted to proceed anyway and circumvent the rules. They figure that, since the land contract is simply an agreement between the two parties, the lender will never know. They're convinced of this because, with a land contract, the seller does not sign the deed for the buyer until the buyer has paid off twenty percent of the purchase price in some states, or the entire amount in others. So many buyers and sellers feel that as long as the deed is not transferred, the mortgage company will not find out. But lenders have ways of discovering underhanded sales; for example, the lenders are always sent a copy of a new insurance policy. If there is evidence of an unapproved land contract sale, they're very likely to call the loan. That would put you, as buyer, in a difficult financial and legal situation, and you'd stand a good chance of losing the property. If the note is called, you'd have to walk away, or buy the property again at less than optimum terms.

When I was an inexperienced investor, I had problems with land contract purchases— not once, but four times— before I learned my lesson to stay away from buying on land contracts altogether. One difficulty arose when I had purchased a property from a lady who was not doing too well with her investments. I should have been wary of this. One particular problem with land contracts is that usually the buyer makes the payment to the seller, and the seller is supposed to make his or her payment to the bank. Most land contracts are written this way. My problem here was that the seller did not make the payments to the bank and, worse yet, she filed bankruptcy. Fortunately for me, her debt balance was very low. The bankruptcy court cut a deal for a cash settlement from me and shaved off much of my balance. So I did manage to come out "smelling like a rose" on this one. But I realize that I was unusually lucky.

My second land contract problem arose as a result of a fire at a duplex, a building with two units, one above the other. It all began when the tenants started to feud. There was a heated exchange in which one tenant waived a pistol at the other. The husband and wife went out that evening but left the teenage daughter to babysit the three small children. Unknowingly of this, the inebriated upstairs tenant allegedly set his upstairs unit on fire and left, obviously to get even with the downstairs tenant. I speculate that he assumed that the fire would engulf the entire building and kill the downstairs tenants. Luckily, a neighbor saw the blaze and saved the four children. No one was hurt.

As I think back, I can recall answering the phone and hearing someone screaming, "Your house is on fire!" I remember replying that I could not see any fire or smoke. After she gathered her wits, she gave the location of that particular duplex that was on fire. The damage really was not that severe. It mostly consisted of broken windows from the firefighters, and smoke damage. I got estimates for the repairs and then made them myself. The insurance company made the check out to me and the seller. This was because the deed was in his name, and I listed him as a mortgage holder. The seller somehow felt that he was entitled to some of those profits because he was the "true owner." Finally, after some legal persuasion from my attorney, he conceded and endorsed the check.

My third unfortunate experience with a land contract purchase occurred when the mortgage company called the note two weeks from the time the land contract was filed. It was in my early days as an investor, but nevertheless I should have known better than to proceed with a land contract purchase without the bank's permission.

Fortunately I had time to acquire bank financing and was able to hang onto the property.

My final run-in with land contracts came when I was selling a property that I had bought two years earlier on land contract. That time I thought I was smart because I personally made the payments to the bank with the seller's payment book. My buyer had loan approval and we were waiting to close the deal. The title insurance company called and said that the original seller needed to sign a document that had been overlooked when I bought it. Naturally, no one could locate her and I was told that if she didn't sign, the closing was off. We searched high and low, and finally managed to locate her in the nick of time. I was lucky. And I was also fortunate that she was willing to sign the document. However, this close call cured me for good. I knew that my luck would eventually run out. Needless to say, that was the last land contract for me.

Even today investors tell me land contracts behind the lender's back are an excellent way to purchase property. They think they have found foolproof ways of keeping the transaction from the lender's notice. Don't believe it! If you follow some of their tactics (for example, not filing the deed or land contract at closing but not filing it, or asking the seller to keep the insurance policy in force), the bank may not know of the agreement between you and the seller, but you are putting yourself in a precarious position. Since there would be no record of your ownership at the courthouse, the seller could refinance or obtain a second mortgage secured by the property. Or someone could slap a lien on "the seller's" property as well. What happens if there is a fire and the seller had cancelled the insurance policy, without mentioning this to you? Any of these could be quite devastating to you, the buyer, especially after you've made extensive repairs or paid a considerable amount of money to the seller. A risk like this is too great for me.

Your goal should be to try to remove the risk from real estate, not increase it. I highly recommend that you avoid purchasing on land contracts, especially those written without the lender's permission. The undercover variety is dangerous and even when there is no existing loan to worry about, your interests would be much better served by a purchase money mortgage or trust deed transaction.

4. HUD and VA Lists

As I mentioned earlier in this chapter, the Department of Housing and Urban Development and the Department of Veterans Affairs offer programs for insuring or guaranteeing loans on many types of housing. When borrowers default on these loans, HUD and VA end up with the foreclosed properties. These are offered for sale and can be an excellent source of property for investors.

The HUD list is found in the real estate section of Sunday papers most cities. Only a quick momentary scan of the list is necessary. Just look for the double address on a street in your predetermined area and check the price. If something interests you, contact your real estate agent for a showing. From the time of the publication of the HUD list, you'll have only a few days to have your agent submit a sealed offer. You must put a $500 deposit down with the offer and the balance is due within thirty days. The highest bid is accepted.

The VA lists have periodically been posted in the local Sunday newspapers. But generally you must check with a real estate agent to find out what is currently available and to inspect the premises. The great thing about this opportunity is that the VA will often finance the property with about $1500 down and at a excellent interest rate. Again, the offer must be submitted as a sealed bid.

There was a time when VA offered a warranty on the heating, plumbing and electrical systems of properties on its list. Not any more! Let me take a moment to apologize to investors, at least those in central Ohio. I accept the responsibility and blame for VA's decision to eliminate its warranty on the mechanical systems in run-down properties in this area. Here's how it happened: I once obtained the highest bid on a property in the southern part of Columbus. I paid a down payment of $1,500 and received financing at an interest rate of nine percent. As in most transactions back then, all of the mechanical systems were included in the warranty.

After the closing, I began the exterior work as usual and inspected the interior to determine the repairs that would be needed. The furnace didn't come on, and half of the electricical system wasn't functioning. On top of those problems, I found extensive leaks in the water lines and drains. When I remembered that all of the systems were under warranty, I called the real estate agency that had handled this VA property and I reminded the agent that, since all systems were warranted, I wanted the necessary repairs to be made. The agency gathered professional estimates from furnace, plumbing and electrical contractors— estimates that the VA considered "absolutely ridiculous." However, the VA did stand by its warranty and, after minimal persuasion, did complete and pay for all of the repairs. However the VA policy was immediately changed and mechanical systems in this type of property are no longer covered by a warranty. I regret that I was the cause of the change, but I'm sure that it was bound to happen anyway.

Even without the warranty, any investor can find it advisable to purchase from the VA lists, since VA offers financing. On the other hand, since HUD requires full payment at closing, only cash buyers will find these deals to their liking.

5. Cash And Short Term Loans

If you are working with cash in hand, you can certainly direct your own destiny. Few finance companies and even fewer banks will loan money on run-down property, but with cash, you are in a strong bargaining position. After all, the sellers of dilapidated property have only three choices: to trade for another property, to finance the purchase themselves or to sell cheaply to a cash buyer. Most sellers would rather cash out.

At a foreclosure sale, cash is your ideal companion. Most foreclosure purchases require a cash deposit of $1,000 to $3,000, with the balance due in thirty days. Without cash savings, you'll have a difficult time buying these bargains. If you have excellent credit you may be able to secure a short-term loan from a finance company, at a high rate of interest, but you'll also need money for repairs. Consider such a loan only if you are buying at a fantastic, rock-bottom price, for example, one third to one half the price you'd normally be able to negotiate. Also be sure that you'll be able to generate money quickly from that property, since you'll be required to send large sums to the finance company to eliminate this high-interest revolving loan.

As an alternative plan, you could make the repairs, then sell the property immediately, for a quick pay-off. One sale like this could possibly give you the money needed to pay cash for the next double. But counting on such a sale to bail you out is risky. If you don't have the cash to buy the building in the first place, you'd be much better off finding a partner with cash and entering into a joint venture to buy the property to keep or resell.

6. Bank Loans

Where investment property is concerned, I am opposed to bank financing on the whole, because of its high cost of origination and lack of assumability. It's probably just as well that I avoid it, because investors specializing in rental properties like mine are not, as a rule, given a warm reception by mortgage bankers.

I find it interesting to note that the properties that make the most profitable investments are in zip codes the banks would like to label "undesirable." In the past, the practice of *redlining*, or refusing to make loans in certain neighborhoods, was prevalent. Today, redlining is illegal, but after many lawsuits and government reprimands, banks have found other ways to accomplish the same results. For example, most mortgage lenders have simply increased the minimum loan amount to $35,000, a practice which disqualifies my properties and virtually all of those within that section of the city.

Even with higher-priced investment property, where a $35,000 loan might be appropriate, purchasers of non-owner-occupied housing must still pay a cash down payment equal to a whopping 30% of the appraised value. In addition, the lender will insist that the building be completely repaired before the loan will be granted. This, of course, defeats your investment plan, so choose alternative methods of financing, such as assumptions or seller-financing where available.

7. The FHA 203k Loan

HUD offers new loans for property requiring extensive repairs. These loans, from what is known as the 203k program, allow a buyer (either an investor or an owner-occupant) to finance the property plus additional repair costs. With this program, the government offers insurance to the lending institution willing to make the loan. 203k loans can be used to finance the purchase price minus the down payment, but plus the total fix-up cost. As each repair is made, a percentage of the loan balance is released to the buyer. Watch out! You can be buried quickly with this type of loan.

Although the 203k is gaining popularity among investors, because it requires a somewhat lower down payment than other investor loans, I still prefer to stay away from banks entirely. I find that there are too many hoops to jump through. The cornerstone to my success strategy has been the maneuverability of buying and selling without the heavy restrictions and high cost of bank loans.

A Summary of Financing Options

If you have little cash and want to utilize my investment strategy, stick to loan assumptions, purchase money mortgages, and VA repossessions. You'll find these to be not only the safest but also the best ways to purchase investment properties.

Financing Down Payments And Repairs

This entire process of accumulating real estate is a very slow and methodical one. In order to maximize your profit and establish a large base income, you must stay dedicated to your primary goal. I strongly recommend that you do not borrow down payment or repair money, except in the quick payback manner that I have described. Instead, fund your repairs and down payments, where possible, from your current income and savings. Postpone personal expenditures until your investments are on a sound footing. This conservative approach will slow your acquisition and repair progress somewhat, but in the long run, your income and overall net worth will far exceed those of other investors who have tried different methods.

Earlier in this book, I demonstrated how you could acquire ten or twenty doubles, work for free, and end up with just the income from one double. Why bother? What is the point of acquiring many properties in a short time if you don't reap the benefits? Instead, own **fewer** properties that make **more** money— that's a much smarter idea. When starting out, decide to own five properties that do quite well instead of ten properties that do not. Or own ten properties instead of twenty. Be determined that the properties you own, whether ten or twenty, should offer you a higher return than the return other investors expect. Reduce your work load by maximizing the profits and the income on each property. By using this method, the accumulation is much slower and you end up with fewer properties, but, in the long run, you amass more profitable ones.

Get Ready to Close the Deal

Once you've determined how you'll finance your acquisition, it's time to write up the offer and close the deal.

Chapter 6 will take you through the closing or settlement process, where you'll sign your name on the bottom line and the property will be yours.

6

Closing
the Transaction

Every investor longs for a smooth and easy settlement, yet stories abound of closing days filled with problems, from minor irritations to full-scale battles. With a little planning, you can eliminate many of the difficulties that so often occur.

Does Your Offer Say What You Want it To?

Most offers to purchase are written on a standard form, which is often called a *Sales Agreement*, an *Offer to Purchase and Receipt for Earnest Money*, or a variation thereof. If you are working with a REALTOR®, he or she may use a form created by the local association of REALTORS®; if you are on your own, you can buy a blank form at an office supply store.

Be sure to read the small print carefully, front and back. Even if you have purchased properties in the past, take time to study it before you sign; the wording on the forms is changed from time to time, to reflect changes in real estate law and practices.

Don't be talked into writing and signing an offer that does not reflect your wishes. Don't let an agent write in a closing date or possession date, for example, that isn't in your best interest, simply because "that's what the seller wants." The offer is your wish list, and if the seller is motivated, you may get exactly what you wish for.

However, remember that if you have not included a request or provision in your original offer and want to add it after the offer has been accepted, you may not be able to talk the seller into allowing it to be included in an addendum. After all, once the offer is signed and accepted, neither you nor the seller are bound to any terms other than those included in the offer.

Give Yourself an Escape Route

When you're writing an offer, always insert a "weasel clause," even if you think you'll never need it. Then if you get a bad case of buyer's remorse, you can put on your weasel shoes and get out of the contract. Typical weasel clauses may incorporate provisions for inspections and financing. Standard blank offer forms frequently contain wording which indicates that the earnest money is to be refunded to the buyer if he or she is unable to obtain financing. However, you may wish to be more specific if a certain type of financing is important to you. Another weasel clause might include a request for a professional inspection, with the provision that the offer is contingent upon the buyer's approval of the results. If you don't approve, the deal is off.

Scheduling the Closing

When the offer has been accepted, you're on your way to the closing table. How long it takes to prepare for the settlement will depend upon several factors:

- Is new bank financing is necessary?
- Or is this a cash deal or a quick assumption?
- Does a land contract need to be drawn?
- Will you want your attorney to review the documents?
- Have you requested the right to have inspections made?
- Are before-closing repairs required for financing?

- Are there any other contingencies that must be met?

- Do escrow officers have a backlog of work?

My Rule of Thumb for Closings

Regardless of what type of property you buy or how much you spend, there are three points to remember:

- Always get the deed.

- Always insist on title insurance, if it is available.

- Always hold the closing at the office of a neutral third party, if this is permitted in your state

---

The Importance of the Deed

If you get the deed in your name at closing and see that it is recorded, you have legal proof that you own the property. How much security this affords you will depend upon the type of deed issued. A *general warranty deed* offers buyers the greatest security, in that the seller (or "grantor") warrants that he or she is legally authorized to sell the property and also guarantees that the property is being sold with no encumbrances other than those listed on the deed. On the other hand, a *quitclaim deed* offers little protection, for the seller makes no guarantees whatsoever. There are other types of deeds also, and legal counsel is certainly advisable.

If you are buying on land contract, laws in your state may govern the preparation of a deed. In some states, the deed is not given to the buyer until the contract is paid off; in other states, there is a delay of months or years before the deed is issued. This can cause serious problems for the investor who may decide very quickly to sell a property, only to discover that the previous owner (the other party in the land contract) cannot be located to sign the deed. It is often possible to have a deed prepared at closing, then held in escrow until needed, but unless you know your options, it will be difficult to avoid problems ahead. As I mentioned in the previous chapter, land contracts can be very tricky. Your attorney can suggest ways to make them safer for you and protect your interests in the transaction.

Insist on Title Insurance

In most states, title insurance has fully replaced the abstract system. As protection, it was customary (and wise) for the buyer to have an an attorney search the chain of title. With title insurance, this is no longer necessary. If you have requested it in the offer, the seller will pay the one-time premium on a title insurance policy to protect you, the buyer, against defects in the title. This gives far more protection than a search by an attorney and, if it is available in your area, should always be requested.

I was especially pleased to have title insurance on one of my properties. In January 1993, I received two real estate tax bills for the same property, which I had purchased a few months earlier. When I called the assessor's office I was informed that I owed $1,067.07 in delinquent taxes. Evidently the previous owner had requested separate tax bills for that double, but I'm not at all sure why. When issuing the policy, the title insurance company checked only the one bill and was unaware of the other. To make matters worse, the missing tax bill included all of the liens and assessments. When I notified the title insurance company, they agreed to pay for the mistake immediately. If I had not required the seller to provide title insurance, but instead had paid an attorney to review the title, it would not have been as easy to collect payment for a mistake.

Hold the Closing on Neutral Ground

Settlement procedures vary widely from coast to coast. In Ohio, for instance, buyers and sellers sit down to-

gether, sometimes with their attorneys, to sign the closing documents at the same time. Yet in many western
states, the buyer and seller may never actually meet. Each
makes a separate appointment with the escrow officer to
sign the papers independently.

Tactically, it's a mistake to close in "enemy territory," so
if you have a choice in the matter, select a neutral meeting
place. If you close at the sellers' attorney's office, for
example, you are at a psychological disadvantage. At the
very least, you'll feel uncomfortable; at the worst, you'll
feel that you must agree to last-minute demands by the
sellers or their attorney—or risk jeopardizing the closing.

A neutral closing officer must act impartially. He or she
must include in the documents only what is on the accepted real estate offer, signed by both parties. It is a
fairer closing procedure for both parties involved. Even
when you are the seller, rather than the buyer, this is a
good rule of thumb to follow. Does that mean that you
should not be represented by legal counsel at closing if
you'd like to have your attorney there? Not at all. In a
complicated transaction that could go awry at the last
moment, it's not a bad idea to have legal advice handy.

Seeking Legal Counsel

When I was a beginning investor, I sought legal advice
every step of the way. Even today, there's still a well-
worn path from my office to my attorney's door. Am I so
incompetent or unsure of my knowledge and skills that
I can't handle simple transactions by myself? Of course
not. But if I'm ever tempted to skip the legal advice and
go entirely on my own, I'm reminded of the actual costs
and potential costs that are affected by my decision. For
a minimal fee, my attorney can review or prepare simple
legal documents. If I economize and skip the consultation, I could find myself in a very costly legal mess. Since
real estate disputes are often expensive to resolve, I frequently seek legal counsel as a preventative measure.

As a general rule, I suggest that investors obtain competent legal assistance in the following areas, both before and after purchase:

- Write up or review offers to purchase.

- Assist in tough negotiations, if necessary.

- Prepare or review land contracts or other seller-financing documents.

- Conduct a title search if title insurance is not available.

- Prepare or review closing documents.

- Review or prepare rental agreements.

- Advise you of landlord/tenant rights.

- Initiate garnishment proceedings.

- File eviction notices.

- Assist a tax advisor in structuring a 1031 exchange.

Experienced investors may not need advice for similar situations that occur later, once the initial consultation has smoothed the way.

Purchase Adequate Insurance

By the day of closing, you'll need to have an insurance policy in place that will protect your building against hazards such as fire and that will offer you adequate liability coverage as well. As a starting point, insure the building for the amount of the purchase price, even if it is currently boarded up. Purchase a minimum of $300,000 liability coverage at the time of closing, then increase this amount to one million dollars worth of liability when the units are ready for renters. Personally, I like a policy with a $1,000 deductible because the rates are cheaper. Since I can make repairs easily for damage from break--ins and other causes, minor repair costs will be taken care of by my monthly maintenance budget. The only claim that I will ever file will be a large fire claim. As with an auto insurance policy, the fewer claims the better.

Insuring high-quality properties has never been a problem. But if you follow my strategy, your investments are likely to be somewhat dilapidated when you first purchase them. It is becoming increasingly difficult to insure these properties and for that reason, I recommend that you deal with two different insurance companies. When one implements a policy change, it is easy to transfer the remaining units to the other agency. Then start looking for another company for new acquisitions or to have handy for some renewals. It will not be easy to establish a lasting relationship with an insurance company. I have found that, with changes in company policy, you may find yourself with a cancellation notice ("We now only insure quality rentals in the nicer end of town.") or higher premiums. Be prepared for this and do not leave yourself vulnerable to this.

Separate and Isolate!

Liability issues extend far beyond insurance matters. New investors should pay particular attention to the deeding of investment properties in order to protect their personal name and other investments.

Before purchasing property, consult with your attorney about the use of trade names under which the deeds would be titled. It is generally safer for investors to own properties by means of Trusts, C Corporations, S Corporations, or Limited Liability Companies, for example, rather than in their own name. Personally, I prefer to invest under the protection of an S Corporation; however, since I am neither an attorney nor an accountant, I am not recommending this or any other type of business entity for you. Your attorney and your accountant can best advise you how to protect yourself and your other investment property from lawsuits. The idea is this: try hard never to be sued, but if you are, lose only what you must.

Understandably, whenever we think of lawsuits, we think of the frivolous type— tenants with ridiculous claims for $85 million because of stubbed toes or the like. Unfortunately, some claims are not so frivolous and we could find ourselves legitimately to blame. Accidents do happen and we must accept the fact that we are at risk.

Separate and isolate! That's my advice to you with respect to liability. What does this mean? It means that once you have a certain number of properties in one entity (an S corporation, for example), you begin another one. This separates the wealth so that all your assets are not piled together under one ownership. If a tenant sues the entity that owns a particular investment, all the other properties in that entity are at risk. By separating the ownership of groups of properties, you are isolating potential problems and limiting your liability. This helps insulate yourself and your other holdings from that lawsuit.

When it comes to investing, you have three vital lines of defence: acting responsibly is your first defence, buying adequate insurance is your second, and separating and isolating yourself and your properties is the third.

The Property Is Yours!

When the closing documents have been signed by both parties and recorded, the property is yours! By this time, you should have a plan of action ready, that will allow you to jump right into the process of repairing and improving your property in order to increase its profitablility. The following chapters will help you proceed in an organized way.

Part IV
Improving and
Maintaining Your
Investments

7

Get Ready to Make Improvements

It seems to be a common impression that investing in low-income housing is inevitably "slumlording," where few or no repairs are made and the property looks rundown inside and out. Unfortunately, in most cases, this is true. The slumlords of today and yesterday are investors who want to buy cheap property in dismal condition. Since they come from the "old school of thought" on investment practices, they believe that all repair costs cut into their cash flow. They feel that their investment ends with the down payment. Their function at this point is just to go out and collect the rent. Similarly, I've found that almost all tenants think that most landlords are concerned solely with making money and avoiding repairs.

If it is your intention to buy and accumulate rental housing in low-income neighborhoods simply to collect rent, you are in for a rude awakening. This investment technique did not work twenty years ago, and it doesn't work today. Before you buy the first property, you must shed this school of thought or you will surely not advance to a higher level of income, better tenant relations, and overall peace of mind.

In order to put things in proper perspective, the investor must recognize and acknowledge the obvious. Properties in these neighborhoods may very likely be fifty to eighty years old. That admission in itself should be argument enough to convince you that you will find it necessary to update the mechanicals (heating, plumbing and electrical systems) and bring everything else up to code. These properties are tired and worn out. They've undergone years of neglect by landlords who've done nothing but suck them dry. Your mission will be to bring them back to life by pumping money into them and completing all the necessary repairs, thereby replenishing and revitalizing the properties for your present and future income.

To justify all of these repairs, you must first buy the property wisely as described in the previous chapters. If you pay too much for the building, the cash flow will be unable to support the repairs. So obviously the repairs will not be made and your investment will be doomed to failure.

Recently I purchased a double and, after one month of intensive repairs, I rented both sides. A few days later, I returned to hang the second water meter. The tenant had a friend visiting, an older man who remarked something about the unfortunate expense of the meter and the new furnace that he had noticed in the basement. My reply was that I didn't mind. "I'm improving my building." I wasn't at all surprised when he turned in disbelief and walked away without making further comment. That I would make improvements beyond the necessary repairs was a concept that he did not understand.

Develop a New Attitude Toward Improvements

Begin now to develop a whole new attitude and fresh outlook that all repairs are really improvements. Admittedly, they really are repairs, but our outlook is to improve the property. So a new furnace is an improvement. A new kitchen floor is an improvement. New carpet is an improvement.

Be Sensible About Improvements

However it is necessary to be realistic, as well, when it comes to making improvements. I recommend that you not buy anything that has been gutted (that is, without wallboard or electric wiring). These repairs are too extensive and costly for our strategy. In addition, expenses such as professional waterproofing in the basement or aluminum/vinyl siding are out of the question. We want to make improvements— but not go overboard. The money you do spend should be spent wisely.

Developing a Skilled Team

It is imperative that before you consider the actual repairs themselves, you focus on the labor used to make those repairs. Just as important as the purchase price is on the cash-flow, so is the cost of all those repairs, which reflect on the cash-flow as well. My first rule of thumb is never to look in the telephone directory when hiring someone to work on your rental property. These businesses may well charge enough to drive you out of the real estate field. If you follow my lead, you will pay only a fraction of the going rate.

For starters, you need good and, in most cases, licensed workers you can rely on to complete and maintain your many projects. If you are just starting out, you may have few, if any, contacts. Before I list for you a number of ways to get to know these private contractors you'll work with, here are interview goals and suggestions for getting the best possible workers at an excellent cost.

To obtain ideal estimates, I suggest that you tell each contractor in your initial contact that you are looking for just one person to do all your work for you in that particular specialty. Mention that once you have established a set price, you will not price shop and you will always call him or her for those particular jobs. Naturally, you will need to discuss price with a number of contractors before you know how to recognize a great price. When you finally meet a good contractor who does a fine job at an excellent price, keep your bargain and call that contractor for all of those particular jobs. When the job is completed and you have satisfactorily inspected the work yourself, make full payment immediately. You will develop an excellent working relationship that will ultimately be in your best interest. In addition, I find that it enhances a relationship to buy lunch for your workers on occasion. As simple and basic as it sounds, good reliable help is one of the main ingredients of your imminent success.

For the most part, pay by the job and not by the hour. If you hire someone to clean out the basement, pay twenty dollars. If your electrician is just installing one hundred amp service, establish one set price for all jobs. Roofers can be paid by the job as well. However, do not pay by the "square" (one square = one hundred square feet of roofing) or they may steal shingles to get paid for laying more than they really did. Pay by the entire roof. If there is a tear-off (removing the old roof), calculate that into the total. Repairs on sheeting and fascia boards should always be included in the total agreed-upon price.

How to Find Contractors

It's a good idea to establish your repair contacts and pricing even before you buy your first property. This will help you in estimating the cost of repairs, so that you can adjust the purchase price according to those repairs. Furthermore, having established your labor pool will enable you to expedite those repairs once the property has been purchased. It is in your best interest to finish the job as quickly as possible. The sooner the work is completed, the sooner you can collect rents. And if the city code inspector has already cited the building, you have a deadline to meet. You'll need to get the work begun immediately, if not sooner!

I bought a double on a Friday under these same circumstances. Evidently, when called by the inspector regarding the repairs, the seller gave him my phone number. My wife received a call on the following Tuesday morning from that same city inspector. He was quite abrasive and asked why the repairs had not been made. She replied, "He just bought it last Friday!" Feeling a little foolish, he slithered back into his hole and gave me a 30-day extension. So beware, if you buy something with city code violations on it, make sure that all of your dominoes are lined up ahead of time.

Ask Other Landlords

Without a doubt, the best way to meet key repair people is to ask other landlords to recommend workers who do excellent work at low prices. In this business it is very common to find contractors who, although licensed, work out of their homes. They do not have the overhead of a commercial building and can often do work for less money while still making a profit. I do not expect anyone to work for free, but I don't want to pay more than I must. There are often many repairs to be made and I want to afford all of them as soon as possible. To do this, I am always trying to keep costs down on the contractors I employ.

Join an Investment Association

If you are a new investor, consider joining an association of other rental property owners. In Columbus, Ohio, for example, we have a number of apartment and investment associations, such as the Real Estate Investment Association (R.E.I.A.). By joining such a group, you'll have an opportunity to meet other landlords and find help in enlarging your labor pool.

The Power of Advertising

Another resource for finding workers is the classified advertising section of your local newspaper. I remember years ago when I had a roof that I wanted to have replaced, but I needed a roofer. The one I had used in the past had stolen some shingles from the last job, so I did not want to use him again. So I advertised in the Sunday paper and I received over one hundred calls. I clearly specified that this was on a "need to roof" basis for my own personal buildings and I would call them only when I needed them. No one cared; they were all out of work anyway. A spot labor situation was not a problem and they understood that this was not a permanent job. I could only immediately hire enough help for that one roof job, buy I did write down the names and numbers of the best prospects. That was seven years ago, and I have not advertised for a roofer since.

From time to time, you can find workers through their advertisement in neighborhood papers. This is a perfect situation when you need tree work or light hauling done.

Be Wary of Walk-in Labor

Sometimes potential workers walk up to your job site and ask for employment. Usually, this caliber of worker is capable only of cleaning out the basement or hauling away trash and household debris. Be cautious of those who state, "I can do it all." I have yet to see one who really can. Also be aware that many of these characters will work for you today and rob you tonight after you have gone home. Others may just wish to look inside to scope out what there is to steal another day.

Ask Your Tenants and Workers

Often your tenants know someone who is just the worker you may need. Even if you're not ready to hire, always take the names and numbers and work up a tickler file. When the need arises, you'll be ready to screen the workers for the best contractor.

When you are hiring, I caution you to be careful of stated qualifications given by nonprofessional workers. Be sceptical; you'll find that most will exaggerate in order to get hired. When you do hire new workers, watch them closely so that if they cannot do the job, you can terminate them immediately.

Once I hired an unknown worker to paint a double. Although he assured me he was a good painter, within the first thirty minutes he had spilled an entire gallon of paint and lost a scraper. Needless to say, he was fired on the spot.

Also ask your current workers if they know someone who is capable of performing a certain task. For example, ask your furnace man if he knows an electrician. Or ask your handyman if he knows a furnace man. Personal referrals are always the best.

The Decision is Yours

One final note before starting the repairs is to remember that this is your property. Although your worker is licensed and may know more than you do, only you will make the final decision as to what method is used to make the repair. Have the contractor discuss his or her different ideas, read mine in the chapter that follows, then be guided in your decision by your common sense and your checkbook.

8

Repairs: Shortcuts and Nifty Tips

W hen it comes to making repairs, I have two guiding principles: I organize my repairs so that I'm getting them done with maximum efficiency (and cost-efficiency), and I take sensible shortcuts wherever I can. In this chapter, you'll find tips to assist you in organizing and shortcutting some of the repairs— where shortcuts are possible and practicable. Obviously, if the kitchen counter top is broken or has a section of it missing, you should simply replace it, but many other repairs can be minimalized if you have learned some nifty alternatives.

Whether your investment property is in Atlanta or Aberdeen, Peoria or Portland, you are very likely to encounter certain typical problems. In my years as an investor, I've been faced with the same repairs many times in different buildings. So here are the best shortcuts I've found for the repair problems you're most likely to meet. I've listed them in the specific order in which the repairs are made, so you'll see exactly how I schedule and handle the work on each building.

Exterior Repairs: The Roof

Your work begins on the outside. If you need to repair or replace the roof, this is where you start. When you make your initial inspection of the property, look at all the second story ceilings to check for water stains. If you have checked the interior before the closing, you will already know if the roof is leaking. Unless it is a new roof and the leak has simply resulted from a chimney that was not flashed correctly, a new roof will be needed. Patching a shingled or slate roof is usually a waste of time and money.

I customarily have all of the old roofing torn off, so I know that all the wood underneath is in good shape. Then, if reroofing is necessary at a later date, I will just reshingle. Most shingles made until recently have been 20-year shingles. Just lately, some companies have begun making 25-year shingles. They cost five dollars more per square but the labor remains the same. Each double that I have roofed has taken between sixteen and twenty-two squares.

Plan ahead. You will need to have electricity available if the old roofing is to be torn off. After the tear-off of both the shingles and gutters, I recommend hanging 1" x 8" boards for the fascia. The gutters are removed because they cannot withstand the beating they will take during the tear-off. I use black shingles on all my properties, for two reasons. First, if there is ever a need for roofing cement on the flashing, the black cement will not be an eyesore, even if the worker is a little sloppy. More importantly, all of the roofs will be the same color, permitting you to use leftover shingles on another job.

When I have an old slate roof that is not leaking, I still tear it off and lay a new roof. I like to know that my roof is in excellent condition before installing those expensive gutters.

Exterior Painting

Just as soon as the roof is finished, apply two coats of paint to the siding. I use white for all of my buildings. Extra white paint in unopened cans can usually be returned to the supplier with no difficulty, or saved for the next job. Even a little comes in handy for touching up a porch when a tenant moves out. Remember that specially-mixed colors cannot be returned. I choose white for another reason also: the caulking I use is white. Since the paint and caulking match, it doesn't matter when you caulk. So it makes sense to me to streamline my operation by painting all my doubles white.

I once purchased three doubles in a row. Originally, one was yellow, one was brown, and the third was grey. Soon all three were repainted white and had my trademark large, black house numbers above the porch area. Another landlord commented, "Why would you do that? They all look like they are owned by the same person" I simply replied, "They are all owned by the same person!"

Please feel free, of course, to use a different color for your roofs and painted surfaces than what I have suggested here. However, I recommend that you choose only a brand and color of shingle that is easily obtained everywhere and that you buy a standard shade of ready-mixed paint, not one that the paint dealer blends especially for you. I do emphasize the importance of uniformity: by using exactly the same materials and colors on all of your units, you will realize substantial savings of both money and time, without sacrificing the quality and attractiveness of your properties.

Repair the Porch and Exterior Doors

While the house is being painted, take time to evaluate and repair the porch and the doors. If the porch posts have deteriorated, replace them with 6 x 6 posts. Just use a jack with a 4 x 4 to hold up the porch roof during replacement. If the porch floor is sagging, jack up the porch floor and prop it up with some cement blocks. Hang 3/8" plywood around the skirt of the porch. If the porch floor is too badly deteriorated for patching, lay 3/4" plywood on the entire surface on top or existing floor. Paint the porch with a grey porch-and-deck paint.

The steps are usually fixed with just one or two boards. However, if they need to be replaced, do so with pre-poured concrete steps. Don't forget the handrails. Insert a 4 x 4 post in the ground with a 2 x 4 as the handrail itself.

Change the Locks

Always put new locks on when you have a vacancy. There is no way to tell how many previous tenants are running around with keys. Hang a combination lock box on vacant apartments to allow reponsible contractors to enter at their convenience, but do not give the combination to spot laborers.

Evaluate the Exterior Doors

Try to salvage the exterior doors. Often the door will appear to be in need of replacement because of heavy damage around the door knob and lock. However, you can purchase a brassplated guardplate that covers both door surfaces and the edge of the door. This repairs split and surface-damaged doors where the disfigurement is around the lock areas only.

If the damage is at the hinges, the door can still be repaired. Remove the inside trim at the hinge end of the door. Now remove the door. Slide in and nail a 1 x 4 behind the area where the hinges were attached, leaving the existing wood door frame. All you need to rehang the door is longer screws to reach the 1 x 4. Then replace the trim. After completing the repair, you may find that it still requires a molding on the exterior, at the two sides and top of the door. You can easily tell if it's necessary by standing inside. If you see daylight around the edges of the door, add a flat 1/4" x 1-1/2" molding.

The doors that must be replaced are often those which don't have a good seal, or those which have been repaired too many times. Often I find that these doors were probably poor quality replacement doors that never fit anyway. If you must buy a new exterior door, buy a flush steel door. It is good, basic, and cheap.

After you have initiated all door repairs nail the rear doors closed for security purposes. Leave about 3/8" exposure at the nailhead for easy removal for contractors.

Also nail the first floor windows closed as well. Upon occupancy, remove all "security nails."

Do not install screen or storm doors. Years ago I installed dozens of doors on both the front and rear of almost all of my units. In less than one year, all but two were demolished. Naturally, the tenants wanted them either to be repaired or replaced at my expense. The doors were neither repaired nor replaced. They were all thrown in the trash. This was truly a learning experience.

Repair the Windows

Replace all broken and cracked glass. Forget the window putty and instead use a good painters' latex caulking. This caulking is easier to remove when you replace the glass again. When you inspect the building, you'll probably find a window or two that needs further attention. Most windows will be the wood double hung type. If the window frame is loose, just use an "L" bracket to fasten it back together. If one side of the frame is completely rotted, find a lumber store that will sell you just that one side. In a building I'm repairing now, the entire bottom part of the window frame is missing. So instead of buying just one side as I recommended in the previous situation, I will buy four sides and "make" my own window.

Another common problem is the window that will not stay up by itself when raised. For this, simply use a window clip on one or both sides, depending on how loose it is. Also be sure that all windows have locks and handles; if not, install them.

It's a good idea to board up excess windows. In most of my doubles, the small rear bedroom has three windows on one wall and three on another. To reduce maintenance, I cover up the three windows on the side of the house, using either plywood or drywall (plasterboard) on the inside, and plywood on the outside, then paint to match. Thieves often enter by the side window in the kitchen of many of my doubles, so now I often board these up as well, for increased security. Another window

I consider covering is the window on the second story landing. Here is a window that gets broken nearly every time someone moves out.

After the plywood or drywall is painted, the covered windows are neither distracting nor unappealing. But before boarding, you might want to swap the better frames with usable windows which have rotted.

Board up all basement windows from the outside. If there is broken glass, board up the inside as well. Most frames are wooden, so this is usually a very quick job. However, on occasion you will find a metal window frame. In this case, you'll need to drill holes through the plywood and frames and attach the covering with sheet metal screws. Paint the plywood the same color as the house or foundation if the foundation is painted.

There are two easy ways to handle window screens. (These are required for Section 8 units.) The first is to buy some removable, adjustable screens. I don't recommend this because the screens are expensive and the tenants might take them when they move. Or secondly, you can buy screening on a roll and some narrow wood molding. For installation, roll out the screen and attach with a staplegun. Nail the wood strips over and at the edge of the screen on all four sides. Now cut the excess. This is very cost-effective for installation, repair, and replacement.

Install the Gutters

At this point, the building is just about ready for professional installation of white, seamless gutters. Install strap-hung gutters to add longer life; invariably, the nailed type comes loose and sags. However, to avoid both theft and damage, you must wait until the building is fully occupied. Avoid any aluminum downspouts at ground level also. To accomplish this, use a 4"-5" plastic pipe from the ground at the front of the building, up to six or eight feet. The gutter installer has a plastic adapter to accommodate your innovative plastic downspout.

Do not tie into an existing ground drain until you first check for stoppage. If it is plugged, all the water will go straight to the basement. You might have to dig from the downspout to the street or sidewalk and install a 4" flexible drain from your new plastic downspout. This gets the water away of the foundation. Feed both the second story and porch gutters into the one plastic pipe on each side.

Other Exterior Repairs

Another place water gets into the basement is at the sides of the building where the concrete sidewalk meets the wall. Often, the walk has settled, leaning toward the foundation. If the lean is slight, you can apply a sloped bead of concrete all along the side of the building and it will eliminate this access.

Make sure that you repair or replace broken and chipped sidewalks. This repair could become a written code violation and is best addressed in the summertime at your convenience. If a city code inspector writes the violation in cold weather, he usually will permit you to make the repairs later when the weather is warm. But this repair is best performed on your own timetable without the pressure of a code letter or weather conditions.

Remove all trees that could cause damage to the building. Some trees will ruin your new roof, crack the basement wall, and cause roots to grow into your sewer line. Also a clump of trees will provide a haven for drug dealers. The ideal situation is to have absolutely no dense vegetation on the lot.

Sometimes I've found it necessary to put railroad ties in the rear to prevent actual parking up to the porch steps. If you shovel a gravel-dirt mix on both sides of the ties, it will be impossible for the tenants to move them.

Now my next job is to add new 6" black house numbers and two new black mailboxes— and the immaculate exterior looks like new! Of course in the pages of my book, it does sound so easy. But if you look at your investment as a project where all repairs are definitely going to be made, there are no surprises, regrets, or unexpected expenses. For those landlords who were hoping for an investment with no repairs, the time and expense of the improvements I've just outlined are a living nightmare. The exterior is usually what most landlords fear the most, particularly the roof. Yet with the right attitude from the outset, this project need not be a fear or nightmare for you.

Scheduling Interior Repairs

It's odd— although the exterior repairs are those most often dreaded by investors, interior repairs are far more complicated and tend to be most often reoccurring. Once you get the outside finished, it is set. On the other hand, the interior is constantly being abused and a frequent turnover in tenants compounds your workload. Every time someone moves, you must go back inside and make sure that everything is perfect again.

There is a certain sequence of events for handling interior repairs efficently. For example, it is important that you complete all the plumbing and electrical work before you do anything else inside, while furnace repair or installation (unless it must be done in a very cold basement or garage) can easily be fit into any convenient slot in your schedule. Before any cosmetic work is begun, you must insure that all the plumbing and electrical services are in top condition. Repair or new installation of either of these can destroy ceilings, walls, and floors. It is senseless to patch walls and paint them, only to have to do it again after the plumbing or electrical repairs are made.

Electrical Repairs

As soon as the exterior is completed, I recommend that you tackle repairs to the electrical system first. Once you've taken a close look at it and it appears that your system is safe, call your local electric company to have it turned on. Then make a list of all the repairs or improvements you want to have done. Check to see if the units have 100-amp service. If not, this will be your electrician's main target. While you're contracting for the upgrade in service, look at your list and ask for a bid to include some of those extra electrical chores as well.

Have the licensed electrician install 220-dryer and range plugs, an outlet for the washing machine, plus a shut-off switch for the new furnace and the 100 amp service. Also make sure that you have a working light switch at the top of the basement steps and that there is additional pull chain lighting throughout the basement.

In many older buildings, there is an insufficient number of outlets. Section 8 requires one outlet in each room and two in the kitchen— and this is a good minimum to follow. Check to see if you at least meet this requirement. Often you will find no outlet in either the bathroom or the small bedroom.

Also common are a great many electrical outlets that are broken or nonfunctional. Sometimes electrical ceiling boxes for light fixtures have never been installed, thereby causing difficulty in hanging and rehanging fixtures. Have your electrician install these. Porch lights are rarely in working condition. Usually, just a change in either the switch or the light fixture will take care of the problem.

All of these items should be on your repair list and should be covered in your initial bid from the electrician. It is better and cheaper for you to address all the electrical problems at the same time. Since you and your electrician will have a copy of that list and cost, there should be no dispute later about the various duties and charges. After a working relationship has been established over the course of several projects, no list will be necessary.

Plumbing Repairs

Similarly, it's a good idea to list all the plumbing problems and attack them in much the same way. Make a complete inspection tour through both units, looking for water leaks, clogged drains, and leaking faucets. These problems are most annoying, but are relatively easy to repair. As a cost-saving measure, however, I do recommend that you find a person who snakes out drains to do only the drain jobs and a plumber to do the others.

Always replace the toilet flapper, then replace the float-ball system with a toilet tank repair valve. This will eliminate any water waste and potential running water. Whenever you have a vacancy thereafter, make it a practice to replace the toilet flapper.

In my old properties, I usually find old 1-3/8" drain lines from the claw-foot bathtub that flow to a lead pipe. As you will soon discover, the replacement standards today are 1-1/4" lines for the bathroom and 1-1/2" for the kitchen. In my city, I know of one small hardware store that carries the 1-3/8" claw-foot drain assembly. This is a little more expensive, but sometimes it is the quickest way to finish the job. Often all that is needed is just one or two parts from this assembly. The rest is saved for the next job. If needed, pick up that hard-to-find faucet for this bathtub as well. With the faucet, purchase two chrome 90-degree adapters to attach the water lines.

Sometimes the 1-3/8" drain pipe sticking out of the bathroom floor is cracked where you tie into it. If it is just slightly cracked, you can still use the assembly I described above, but you must utilize a 1-1/4" rubber adapter. Even though the 1-1/4" rubber opening is larger, it will tighten down and become watertight. However, if the 1-3/8" pipe is badly deteriorated, you must go under the bathroom floor or in the ceiling below to saw off behind the damaged pipe. Tie into the lead pipe with a 1-1/2" rubber adapter and 1-1/2" plastic pipe out the other. Send the pipe up to the bathtub drain. If you prefer, you can install the cheaper 1-1/2" plastic drain on the old claw-foot bathtub. As for any repairs, the choice of materials and procedures is up to you. The plumber does only as you instruct; you are in charge. Don't simply ask your contractor to "just fix it." Find out how your plumber plans to make the repair and then decide if that method is best in the long run and most cost-effective for you.

Bathroom Sinks

The bathroom washbowl in an older building is usually a large wall-mounted type without a cabinet. Although these basins are old, I often find them in perfect condition since they're nearly impossible to break or deteriorate. You will, however, often have to install two new single faucets and a drain assembly. Again, it is very difficult to find a drain that will fit a sink like this. If your fixtures are of similar vintage, the type of drain you'll need comes in two parts. One fits in the sink itself; the other comes up from the bottom of the sink where the top part screws down inside the bottom section. Unfortunately, the type that is readily available is a one-piece unit that slides through the sink and is secured with a nut underneath. The problem is that the new drain assembly is too large to fit through the opening of the outdated sink. There is no way to make the new version fit, but you may be lucky enough to find a "hole in the wall" hardware store that still carries your type of rare, old sink drain.

If the washbowl is missing or needs to be replaced, you can purchase a new, smaller wall-mounted sink. The new-style drain does fit this model. And, instead of the single faucets for hot and cold, you will be able to use a one-piece faucet for both.

Never buy a sink top with a cabinet underneath, even if you think that it's more attractive. Every one that I have installed over the years was soon either missing its door-front or had to be replaced with a wall-mounted unit because the cabinet was broken by the tenant. When I install a new sink, I like to finish the job with two additional details. First, I install a 3/4" quarter-round molding across the top to help secure the sink to the wall, and finally I install two legs under the sink at the outermost corners from the wall.

Toilets

I know you'll come across units where the toilet is leaning because of rot in the wood floor underneath. Usually you can fix this by taking a small section of 3/4" plywood and piece of linoleum and placing them directly underneath as a platform for the toilet. Attach the plywood to the floor with 2" wood screws. A plastic flange, available at all hardware stores, will be set through the hole in the platform, into the drain, and will secure the toilet as well. Always use the wax ring that comes with the plastic sleeve, not one without the sleeve. In most cases, this little trick sets the toilet upright and eliminates the need to plywood the entire bathroom floor. Remember, this entire project is yours and it is up to you to cut repair costs whenever possible.

Rarely will the toilet be leaking from the drain pipe leading away from it, but if this happens, here is a handy shortcut to know. Saw and cut out a very small section of pipe and slide in a rubber adapter. Likewise, if the bathtub or washbowl drain is leaking underneath the floor, you can buy rubber adapters for these. You can also purchase multi-sized adapters as well. If a length of pipe is bad, you can replace it with plastic pipe with rubber adapters at both ends. Even though you are not doing the plumbing yourself, you can remove the area of ceiling so that you can diagnose the problem and know how to fix it. Unscrupulous plumbers have been known to earn a whopping fee from owners who are unaware of how simply this repair can be made. Rather than replace everything, a quick patch job will easily suffice. Discuss the repair with your plumber, let him know of your expertise, and he'll give you an excellent price.

If a drain leak happens to be relatively small and is on a surface that you can reach, you can usually buy an epoxy cement to patch it. The best type comes in one package with the two ingredients individually wrapped. First clean the surface with emery cloth or steel wool. Open both packages of epoxy and remove half from each. Mix them together well. The directions indicate that you should apply the mixture to the surface but I've found that this a mistake. Instead, take a little water and wet the exterior of your epoxy mixture. Now take a very small portion and actually try to work it inside the crack with your fingers. Work it in a couple of times. Check to see if your mixture is still moist (if not, just moisten again) and apply it now. Work in the entire amount as if you were trying to get it all in that little crack, then smooth it out and make a bulging surface. If the leak is small, reachable and patchable, this is the best method of repair. Try this tip first, before calling the plumber.

Incidentally, when you are paying a plumber to make repairs, have everything torn out so that there is clear access to the repair before the plumber arrives. If drywall repair is necessary, don't contract with the expensive plumber for this. Just about any handyman can replace what you have torn out. It's a good idea to wait about a day or two before putting ceilings back. You want to make sure that this leak has been stopped and no others have developed.

Note: You'll find a handy checklist of problem-solving techniques for toilets on the following page.

Miscellaneous Plumbing Problems

Often the door to the hot water tank is missing. Just take a sheet of thick tin and cut two slits on each side for a flexible fit for the new door.

Make sure that there are faucets and a stand-up pipe for the washer hook-up to the drain. This is a good time to see if the basement floor drain itself has a cover; it should.

Water Meters

Most doubles will have just one water line coming in from the street and one city water meter. Check to see if there is a company in your city that sells and reads water meters and bills tenants monthly for a small fee, as a service to landlords. They can often be found through

Do-It-Yourself Toilet Problem Solving

Securing the Toilet

A. Toilet leaking around base:
1. Replace wax ring with a new wax ring w/sleeve.
B. Toilet leaking around base and loose at floor:
1. Replace wax ring with a new wax ring w/sleeve and tighten or install new bolts.
2. Check toilet bolts for a good connection in the closet flange. Often the existing metal closet flange (ring that secures toilet to floor) is rusted on one side that securely holds one of the toilet bolts in place. Replace that rusted flange with a new plastic one and secure to floor. Now set new bolts and new wax ring w/sleeve.
C. Closet flange won't secure to floor:
1. Level floor by replacing new floorboards under toilet area.
2. If entire bathroom floor is not level, either lay 3/4" plywood over the entire bathroom floor or utilize the toilet area platform method.

Repairing a Running Toilet

1. Have tenant remove cloth tank cover if holding lever down.
2. Have tenant remove bowl cleaner inside tank if obstructing movable parts.
3. Add slack in flapper chain if too short; replace flapper if old.
4. If ballcock is malfunctioning, eliminate ballcock system and replace with a watersaver toilet tank repair valve.
5. If flush valve is slide type and not sealing tank, replace with flapper system.

Unplugging a Stopped-Up Toilet

1. Plunge aggressively with a good plunger.
2. Snake with a special toilet snake, a two-person job.
3. Pour a 5-gallon container full of water into the bowl. An empty drywall compound bucket works best.
4. Remove toilet and turn it upside down; snake through the toilet bottom, tugging back and forth.
5. Pour a bucket full of water through the bottom of the toilet while the snake is in place.
6. Remove the snake and pour 2 buckets of water through the bottom of the toilet.
7. Turn toilet right side up; pour 1 bucket into the bowl.
8. Again pour 2 more buckets into the toilet bottom.
9. If this fails, call a drain-rooter company or buy a new toilet.

advertisements in the investment section of your Sunday newspaper. If so, purchase and install a second water meter at all of your locations. This minimizes your expenses and, if the tenants are paying the bill, it reduces tenant water waste. If there is a leak, the tenant will be more apt to tell you. Also, if you are currently billed by the city and pay quarterly, you'll find that the tenants' monthly bills (sent from the reading service and paid to you) will reflect water leaks more quickly than a quarterly bill.

To determine where to hang your second meter, go to the basement where there is no meter and find the spot where the water line crosses over. Hang the additional meter there. From this meter, have a second remote outside meter run. When the new outside meter is installed, go to each remote and mark the address of each apartment with a permanent felt-tip marker. Make sure yourself that the readings on both meters and remotes correspond to their respective units.

Outside Faucets

If there are any outside water faucets, consider eliminating them. I do, immediately. If they are left in place, every relative and friend your tenant has will be washing a car here at your expense and neighborhood children will be playing in the water in the summertime. Not having outside faucets and having the tenant paying for water use monthly eliminates most of the water bill problems. Since payments for high water bills are nearly impossible to collect, you must assist in reducing water usage.

The Furnace and Thermostat

Turn on the gas and evaluate the status of the furnace and thermostat. If the pilot light stays on when the furnace fires up and down, and the fan comes on and off by itself without obnoxious noises, you are probably in good shape. However, if the furnace is an old "octopus" type and you have made contact with a furnace contractor whose prices are reasonable, it's a good idea to replace it now and get it over with. Remember, with my investment strategy, I recommend that you keep everything that you buy. From experience I can assure you that furnaces never fail to go out of order on a weekend in the dead of winter! While replacement of an old but functional furnace might seem a little drastic to most investors (and perhaps it is a bit excessive), you must realize that I really do not want to be called out for anything. So I consider this type of preventive maintenance well worth the cost. To me, a furnace that is perhaps sixty years old, inefficient and difficult to repair is a nightmare just waiting to happen. This is my own personal quirk; I have yet to find an investor or even a furnace contractor who understands my eagerness for this expenditure.

It is inconceivable to me that I would be considered a maverick because I make all of these repairs. It seems to me that the reverse would be the case. Actually, in many cases, my repairs barely extend past the city code. But I do admit that replacing a working furnace and nonleaking roof is a bit unusual.

If you do decide to replace the furnace, make sure that all the ductwork in the basement is replaced as well, to improve the efficiency of the furnace. I always request that the thermostat be the round Honeywell model, designed for heat only. The cheaper version that I specify mounts on a clear plastic base, not the large gold colored mount. It is durable and easy to replace. Again keep the policy of uniformity in your thermostats as well. If replacement is necessary, I need only to loosen three screws and remove the thermostat itself. The tiny plastic holder on the wall remains. I simply attach the new thermostat with the three screws inside it.

Whether or not you change the furnace, some small repairs are often needed. Before you call an expert, there are a few things that you can check. If the furnace is not working, first make sure that the circuit-breaker and furnace switches are on. Next, to detemine whether or not the thermostat is faulty, remove the thermostat entirely from the wall. If the furnace comes on when the thermostat wires are touched together, replace it.

On a gas furnace, if the pilot light will not stay on, install a thermocouple. If you have a newer high-efficiency furnace that does not have a pilot light, there might be air in the line. Just flip the furnace switch off and turn the thermostat all of the way down. Now flip the furnace switch back on and then turn the thermostat back up. This eliminates air from the gas line.

If the furnace is still not working, you might want to check the thermostat wire itself from the furnace, and look for anything loose on the furnace. I once had a tenant who cut the thermostat wire to use as a clothes line, so it is now something I definitely check.

Note: You'll find a handy checklist of problem-solving techniques for furnaces on the following page.

Interior Walls

Now that all of the mechanics of your building are in order, we can move on into the cosmetic phase of the interior repairs. You'll find that this phase is the quickest, cheapest, and easiest of all.

Begin installing drywall wherever necessary and by patching the walls in the entire apartment, including the basement stairwell. Remove all nails, tape, and staples from the walls and woodwork at this time. Be sure to inspect and repair the closets for pealing and cracking.

Closet Rods

Very likely there are no clothing rods in the closets; they have a habit of disappearing. Purchase galvanized 3/4" water or gas pipes and cut to fit. Carve half moons in 1 x 4 boards that are 6" long to hold the "clothing rod" in place.

Do-It-Yourself Furnace Problem Solving

GAS FURNACES

Pilot Light Off; Won't Light Or Ignite

A. If standing pilot type:
   1. replace thermocouple.
B. If electronic ignition:
   1. Purge line:
      a. flip the furnace switch to Off.
      b. turn the thermostat all the way down.
      c. flip the furnace switch back to On.
      d. turn the thermostat back up.
   2. Check to see that furnace switch is On.
   3. Check fuse box or circuit breaker.
   4. Check thermostat by touching wires together. If the furnace comes on the thermostat needs replaced.
   5. Check entire thermostat wire; could be loose at furnace or thermostat, or have line cut.
   6. Close bottom furnace door to engage safety switch.

Pilot Light Is On, Furnace Won't Kick In

A. If standing pilot type:
   1. Check gas control valve to see if it has been turned from Pilot to On. (It really happened to me.)
   2. Check furnace switch for On.
   3. Check fuse box or circuit breaker.
   4. Check thermostat by touching wires together. If the furnace starts, thermostat needs to be replaced.
   5. Check entire thermostat wire; could be loose at furnace or thermostat, or have line cut. (Once I saw it used as a clothes line.)
   6. Close bottom furnace door to engage safety switch.
B. If electronic ignition; novice can't handle these repairs.

ELECTRIC FURNACES

Pilot Won't Ingite

1. Check to see that furnace switch is On.
2. Check fuse box or circuit breaker.
3. Check thermostat.
4. Check entire thermostat wire.
5. Close bottom furnace door to engage safety switch.

Doorknobs

Doorknobs are always missing. Although these are usually the old type, they can be bought just about anywhere. There is a certain kind of replacement knob that I have discovered is best, however it's difficult to find. Most doorknobs screw on and then tighten down with one screw for each knob. (This is why the knob is missing in the first place.) The replacement knob I suggest has two screws at each end and tightens down very securely. All of these knobs which I have used as replacelments are still on the doors.

Doorstops

Doorstops are another one of my pet peeves for which I finally found a solution. For years I have installed the purchased variety that is brassplated and screws into the baseboard. Although they are very inexpensive, it is a frustrating hassle to keep installing these doorstops for the same doors every time someone moves. In the upstairs rooms, I now cut a small section of 2 x 4 and nail it to the floor, baseboard, or to the inside bottom of the door. I have yet to find one of these missing or broken when I redo an apartment.

Bathroom Walls and Floor

Whenever you have a modern-style bathtub that is flush with the wall, it behooves you to install some type of waterproofing on the wall. I recommend a waterproof bathtub paneling product that is sold in a 4' x 8' sheet. Cut down the sheet to a size that is two feet high and the length and widths of the tub, to fit around the bathtub walls. This will prevent wall deterioration and leakage to the kitchen below it. After affixing it to the wall with the recommended adhesive, thoroughly caulk the tub and paneling seams to reduce leakage.

The bathroom floors (and platform if applicable) will have a one-piece sheet vinyl— not tile— laid on them. Buy this in a 6' x 9' roll at a building supply store. This will help waterproof the floors from toilet and bath water overflows. Heavily caulk at the floor area around the water and drain lines and at the baseboard to help in the waterproofing battle.

The Kitchen Floor

The kitchen floor usually requires an underlayment of 1/4" lauan plywood. For a floor that will endure the dragging of the heaviest refrigerator, I recommend 1-ft. square tile a full 1/8" thick. This is what commercial establishments use to accommodate heavy traffic, and I've found that we need this floor for our tenants. To find it, go to a flooring store that caters to contractors. Ask at the counter about their close-outs and choose a tile from them. This will save about twenty dollars per kitchen. The average kitchen floor in my doubles will require three to four boxes of tile. Most tile stores will allow an unopened box to be returned, but check the store's policy before buying. This type of floor will be glued down, and you'll need a quart of adhesive for a standard kitchen floor.

Handrails

Make sure that all handrails are in place before you get ready to paint. Install a 2 x 4 handrail in the basement and, at the same time, check the steps and replace where needed. Insure that there is a 2 x 4 brace under those steps. Now check the handrail going to the second story. If it is missing, buy an attractive, unfinished handrail that can be stained. If the existing handrail is loose, remove it and attach a 6" to 8" square piece of 3/8" plywood to the wall with 2" wood screws. Now reattach the handrail to the plywood.

Pocket Doors

If there are sliding pocket doors between the living and dining rooms, push them inside the wall and plywood over them. They will not function with carpet and repairing broken tracks for tenants can be a nuisance. Also if there is a door going from the dining room to the kitchen, remove it as well. You'll be eliminating a possible repair call by removing it. Do save the door though, for a future door replacement need.

Attics

If there is a stairwell to the attic and the floor joists are wide enough to meet building code requirements, then you should refinish the attic. Section 8 may pay $100 more per month per unit for the fourth bedroom. Install a new window and frame up for walls and a flat ceiling. Have the electrician install a ceiling light and outlets. The furnace contractor can easily install a gravity floor register for heat. When the work is completed, carpet the stairs and the attic itself to make it a fabulous fourth bedroom.

Interior Painting

Check the entire unit for water stains on walls and ceilings. Wherever they are found, apply a good water stain primer over those areas before painting. For small stains, use a spray can of white primer. Now you're ready to paint the entire apartment white. After two coats, the unit will really start to sparkle. When all the walls are completed, I paint the wooden floors upstairs and the steps themselves with a dark brown oil-base porch-and-deck paint. I also paint the little alcove at the top of the basement steps and the furnace grates.

Carpet

Install carpet in the two downstairs units only. If there is a tiny hallway in front of the basement door, leave that uncarpeted. The washing machine and dryer would surely tear the carpet when they're being moved to and from the basement. In most of my doubles, these two rooms require approximately 40 sq. yards of carpet.

The Final Touches

When you go back in to give the apartment a final inspection, fine-tune the unit by adding smoke detectors and a new furnace filter. Loosen any windows that have been painted shut, and install latches for the basement and master bedroom doors. Recheck the toilet for possible adjustment. Attention to little details like this make the unit safe, efficient and pleasant to live in. You'll gain a sense of pride and accomplishment when the job is completed. Later, when you show the apartment, the prospective tenants will be amazed at how great the unit looks. They are clearly not used to finding rental property in such well cared-for condition.

Making Repairs After Destructive Tenants

Tenant damage is an ongoing and eternal problem. To eliminate a massive build-up of damage and destruction you must make the repairs immediately and give the tenant a bill. The bill will specify that the tenants have only have 30 days to pay in full or you will demand that they move. This usually will get you paid but probably will not eliminate future damages caused by these tenants. However after a few of these episodes, they'll get tired of paying your repair bills and will eventually decide to move.

When tenants complain to the code enforcement bureau, you'll also have to answer to the city inspectors. Believe me, I am most assuredly no fan of the city code inspectors. Most of those I have encountered have been arrogant and have enjoyed wielding a sense of power from their lowly position. Furthermore, they often do not understand that tenants can be very destructive. Years ago I was confronted by an inspector who was upset when he saw a three-foot-square hole in the wall. He asked, "How do you expect these people to live like this?" He seemed to be implying that I had either done the damage myself or, at the very least, let them move in with the wall damaged. When I insisted, "It wasn't like this when they moved in," my answer fell on deaf ears. He actually threatened to send me to jail. Eventually, I evicted the tenants, made the repairs and did not go to jail. I continued to buy plenty of rental property. And he remained a lowly inspector.

Recently when I went to acquire a roof permit from the city, I noticed an adage posted on the wall. "Dealing with an inspector is like wrestling in the mud with a pig. After a while, you realize that the pig enjoys it." How appropriate!

When you are dealing with destructive tenants, it is important to remember that you must take the situation in hand swiftly, before the damage escalates. Have the tenants reimburse you for the unit's immediate repair and, if the damage is likely to continue, insist that they move. You do not need tenants who are trying to destroy what you have built.

Sprucing up For the Next Tenant

Earlier in this chapter I stressed that uniformity is essential for cost-effective improvements. It also is an excellent way to ease your future repair burdens. For example, when a tenant moves out, I can generally repaint the entire unit in thirty minutes, with less than one gallon of paint. Because I use exactly the same paint that was used earlier, all I need to do is to paint the wall up about three feet high, using only a paint roller. Usually, no brush is needed. This takes care of the hand prints and freshens the walls beautifully. I recommend that you purchase your paint from an established paint store and stick with it. You'll be buying paint each time from the same manufacturer and therefore the colors will remain the same. Even the white paint I use must match up perfectly in order to avoid painting every square inch. Did you know that there are over 300 shades of white paint on the market? For quick touch-ups, such as a porch or even just the front door, an accurate match is a great time- and money-saver.

When a tenant moves out, inspect the unit in its entirety. First repair any obvious damage. Touch up the paint throughout, as I mentioned above, then clean the carpet. Change the locks, the furnace filter and the toilet flapper. Check the smoke detectors for batteries. Now you're ready to hang your sign and place your advertisement, as we'll cover in the following chapter, when we take a look at several of the best ways to attract and keep reliable tenants.

Part V
Managing
Your Rentals

9

Renting Your Units

Since income from your rental properties is your primary investment goal, your ability to find suitable tenants for your units will determine how quickly you attain that goal. So read this chapter carefully.

Effective Advertising

As soon as the unit becomes vacant, post a For Rent sign. Tape it inside the front window or, when possible, nail the sign outside, up high on the porch exterior. Be sure to remove all curtains to enable prospects to peek into the windows. However do not buy paid advertisements until the unit is ready.

When you have completed the necessary repairs, advertise only in the Sunday paper, and keep it brief. I've found that a simple two-line classified is the most cost-effective form of advertising. Don't waste money on fancy descriptions when it is imperative to keep expenses down and enhance your cash flow.

In your advertisement, specify the area, address, number of bedrooms, type of unit, rental amount, and phone number. If there is any space left, insert the words "carpet" or "appls," if applicable. Here's an example of a perfectly complete and succinct ad. While it won't win a Pulitzer Prize, it always gets results for me.

NE 0000 Cleveland Ave, 3 br, 1\2
dbl, carpet, 325 mo, 000-0000.

On the Sunday your ad is running, make yourself available to answer the responding telephone calls. Many tenants do not have a telephone, so obviously you cannot return their messages. If you must be away from your telephone that day, a call-forwarding option on your phone may come in handy. Or ask someone else to field your calls.

Screening Prospective Tenants

If the caller is familiar with the neighborhood and has a full cash deposit, set a time for the showing as soon as possible.

If you screen your tenants too well, all of your units will remain vacant. In the type of neighborhood I recommend as excellent investment territory, your units will be "low-income" housing— and low income means exactly that. It is unrealistic to assume that a welfare recipient is going to meet all of his or her financial obligations on a welfare check. It is more accurate to assume that most tenants in this price range do have bad credit and will eventually not pay rent. If you adopt this philosophy, it will encourage you to conduct yourself in a highly protective, methodical, and legal manner.

When a prospective tenant calls in answer to your ad, discuss the precise location of the unit. If the prospect is still interested, inform the caller that a full deposit is required. These two steps are absolutely essential. As soon as you answer the phone, you must quickly weed out those not interested in that area and those trying to reserve an apartment with little or no deposit. Be prepared: nearly everyone will want you to hold the unit with no cash deposit. Your reply must be absolutely firm: do not be talked into holding a unit without money down. The first one with the cash gets the apartment. Emphasize that this is to be rented on a "first come, first served" basis.

Don't Allow Pets

Pets would be all right if tenants took care of them, but they often don't. Unfortunately, the landlord is left with a smelly basement to cleanup and suffers the cost of flea extermination, a fee which alone ranges from $175 to $875 for a full elimination. A "no pets" rule helps prevent exhorbitant maintenance work and cost.

Be Firm About the Cash Deposit

Never meet prospective renters at the apartment unless they have a cash deposit or unless they need a statement for a financial assisting agency (I'll tell you more about that later in this chapter). Your time is very valuable, so do not show the apartment twenty times to people without money. If a caller is due to get a check on Friday, schedule the showing at that time. Remember, he or she can always give the unit a drive-by in the meantime and peek in the windows.

Many callers will want to "work something out" for the deposit. They'll assure you that they can fix or repair anything. Coincidently, they'll be sure to tell you that they are professional painters, carpenters, roofers, or whatever skilled help it appears that you need at that time. You cannot afford to be soft. Nip this in the bud immediately by a quick reply, "No deals." Income from your rentals is your primary goal and to make this system work, you must receive full rent and deposit. If the unit is in tip-top condition (as it should be if you've followed my recommendations), you deserve to be paid well for it.

Occasionally I can't resist the temptation to follow through with this conversation. So I ask a prospective tenant just what he would like to do. He will invariably look around and find nothing legitimate (after all, it's been thoroughly redone). But this doesn't stop him.

"I could paint," he suggests.
"I just applied two coats of paint," I say.
"Yeah, but I don't like white," he continues.

At this point, his girlfriend looks at me and we both shake our heads at how absurd the conversation has become. He notices this at last and just laughs. Well, at least he tried.

Other Ways to Attract Tenants

While advertising (either by a sign on the building itself or an ad in the Sunday classifieds) should bring plenty of prospective tenants your way, don't overlook other sources of renters and rent money that are available to you. The neighborhoods and doubles I have recommended to you as excellent investment potential are just the type of rental units that many government agencies and private organizations are seeking to house needy families. Don't be too quick to dismiss this idea, if the thought of renting to indigents concerns you. Some of my best renters have appeared in this way and, after you read the next several paragraphs, you may be surprised at the benefits such an arrangement can offer you.

Children's Services as a Source of Renters

The state Children's Services division can often play an important role in renting your units. Develop a working relationship with the counselors. Advise them that they can give prospects your name and phone number anytime, now and in the future. When the client calls, you can explain what is available.

I have found that, depending on the client's paricular situation, Children's Services will pay anywhere from one-half to two months' rent. Most of their "families" consist of an adult female with children, either from a homeless shelter or currently being evicted.

These are undoubtedly some of the most desperate tenants available. But, believe it or not, the majority of these people make great renters! There are two reasons for this: first, they desperately need housing and second, they will have Children Services counsellors keeping tabs on them. Since many of them have very recently been evicted, they have firsthand knowledge of what happens to them when they become "nonpays".

If your tenant starts backsliding, you have a contact whom you can call on for assistance. Contact the Children's Services representative who met you originally and handed you the rental check. That representative will help the tenant find a way to pay the rent that is due or may assist the tenant in getting out of your unit in a timely fashion. As you will see in the Chapter 10, this assistance in removing the tenant saves you money in attorney and court costs, bailiff tag and set-out fees, and makes the unit available much sooner. This helps prevent the unfortunate situation where a nonpaying tenant stays in the unit until the last minute, and is evicted at considerable cost to you.

When you rent to a client of Children's Services, it is essential that you still get both rent and deposit before any lease is signed and keys are given. Even if the Children's Services representative tells you that the check will be mailed on Friday, stick with your policy. I've found that after the tenant moves in, agencies tend to lose interest in the arrangements. It's not uncommon for them to change the dollar amounts which you have previously agreed to. My stringent policy has not prevented me from renting my units and, furthermore, it motivates the agencies to expedite the paperwork (i.e., your check). When you hold firm, they readily agree that the tenants have waited this long, so certainly they can wait until Monday to sign the lease and move in.

Section 8 Housing Brings Benefits

Section 8 housing is privately-owned housing that is sponsored and subsidized by government money. The Section 8 agency has its own department located within your local Metropolitan Housing Authority. As I mentioned earlier, Section 8 rentals can be very profitable, if you're willing to jump through a few hoops to get them.

About two weeks before your unit is ready, call Section 8 and place it on the "apartments-available" list. Give the address, number of bedrooms, your name and phone number. For speedier results, take a picture of the building and beside it, tape the rental information. Post this on the bulletin board at the Section 8 office.

When prospective tenants call from the listing, be sure the callers have a "certificate" in hand before you schedule a meeting. If they don't have the certificate (necessary for all Section 8 rentals), you will most assuredly be wasting your time. Often people like to shop around to see what kind of units will be available to them, when it could be weeks, or even months, before they actually obtain one. But if your prospective tenants have the certificate already and want to rent the unit, fill out the certificate for them to return to Section 8. Tell them that if they want you to hold the apartment, they must submit it immediately and must call you when they have turned it in.

With Section 8 rentals, the deposit amount is calculated by the agency. In almost every case, the amount is less than half the rent. This is acceptable to me because there are guaranteed rent and damage provisions in their leases which compensate for the lower amount I'm holding. Although the tenant pays the deposit, the agency generally pays all of the rent. Occasionally, there will be a partial rent paid by the tenant, based on financial circumstances. Obviously, as a landlord, your best arrangement is where Section 8 pays the entire portion. In that case, the Metropolitan Housing rental check is mailed directly to you.

After the certificate has been turned in, a Section 8 inspector will call to set an appointment for inspection. If the unit is not ready yet, stall the appointment. If you've followed my repair recommendations in Chapter 8, the unit will be in excellent condition at time of renting, with no city code violations. However, with this agency, you must go just a bit further with the following additions:

- All utilities must be turned on at the time of inspection.

- There must be at least one window screen for each room.

- All basement electrical outlets and switches that run down from the ceiling must be in conduit.

The rents do not start until after the inspection has been made and you'll have no tenant if the unit fails. However, although the Section 8 Housing process is slower and riskier, the benefits for you may outweigh its drawbacks. For example, Section 8 will pay and guarantee one year's rent. The check will be mailed to your post office box about the fourth of every month. This eliminates the need for rent collection.

As you recall, there was a move-in inspection. If the tenant leaves and the unit is trashed, the damages are easily traced to the tenant, through a move-out inspection by a Section 8 inspector. There used to be a certain procedure which you followed in filing a damage claim, but as of October 1, 1995, this became the tenant's responsibility. I suggest that you still pick up a copy of a move-out inspection when your first Section 8 lease is signed. When someone moves out, be ready to list the damages and mail it to the ex-tenant.

Every year, with Section 8 rentals, the tenant and landlord must agree in order to continue the lease. If both are in agreement, there are provisions that call for annual inspections as well as an increase in rent. The owner need not be present for those subsequent inspections; Section 8 makes the appointments with the tenant and mails the results to the owner. If the unit passes, an increase is usually granted. If not, a list of necessary repairs will be sent. You will have thirty days to make the unit acceptable for an additional inspection. If the unit fails again, you will either experience a rent reduction or cancellation.

Nonprofit Organizations Need Units

In every city there is at least one large nonprofit organization that is very effective in helping those in dire need obtain housing. You might find such an organization in your city through a casual discussion with an agent of another agency, or by actually receiving a check from that agency. In the latter case, when you go to verify tenant information with the organization, discuss with them in detail about their particular function and find out exactly how they financially assist the needy.

In Columbus, there is an organization called the Interfaith Hospitality Network. This network is compiled of sixty-seven local churches, many of which are in excellent uptown neighborhoods and yet are committed to helping homeless families. All the funds are obtained from the donations of congregations and church fund drives. There is no federal, state, or local funding for this project.

For this particular organization, the only criterion for "family" is that there must be a child in it. It is this agency's function to house these families at first through Day Centers during the day and in local church buildings at night for as long as thirty- to forty-five days. During this time, they actively seek housing for them.

The usual assistance includes one full month's deposit to be paid for this prospective tenant. However, when the church is actively involved with the family, it may pay the entire rent, deposit and more. They do not want this particular family's situation to deteriorate any further. Their contention is that once families dip too low in society, it will be more difficult to help them work their way back into functioning family units.

This agency— and others like it in cities across the U.S.— would welcome your vacant units and will aid in occupancy. Organizations like this have an unbelievably difficult time in placing families because of strict rental guidelines. In fact, even low-income housing agencies run by the government often refuse these tenants because of bad credit and bad rental history. This fact, I find particularly surprising.

Other organizations offer similar services on a smaller scale. For example, the Volunteers Of America assists in some immediate housing and finds permanent rental housing for families. In Columbus, Ohio, they own twenty-five units that they utilize for temporary housing. While living there, each family must save half of their income, which is actually held by the VOA. When enough money is saved, the tenant has a check cut for the new landlord. The VOA also assist in furniture for each family, but the money that you, as a landlord, will receive is entirely the tenant's own. The organization itself has no funds for rent, deposit, or utilities, however, they occasionally help place a family with another organization for additional help.

In Columbus, the Volunteers Of America organization publishes a weekly newsletter, listing available housing. I call them when vacancies arise and place my units on the list. Again, this agency has credit and reference problems with their tenants, so they welcome your vacancies.

Welfare: A Rental Resource

The state welfare department can play a role in renting your units as well. For many tenants, welfare will pay the deposit, while the tenant must provide the first month's rent. Beware of tenant statements about the approval of welfare assistance. The welfare department will usually give a prospective tenant a paper for the landlord to fill out. Just because you fill it out, and a dollar amount is specified on it, it does not mean that a check will be mailed to you. Many claims are denied even after the landlord has filled out the information.

Another type of assistance is available also. If individuals are receiving Aid for Dependent Children, they are eligible for emergency aid once a year. If it is used on a $40 electric bill, for example, then they may not ask for emergency assistance again for one full fiscal year. However, most welfare recipients have discovered that it's best to use this service when they are in rent or gas default, or for more expensive debts. This service is used by renters either to try to stay at the present address (if the landlord will accept a late rent check) or to move elsewhere.

Get Rent and Deposit up Front

Be sure that you have received both the rent and deposit before the lease is signed and the keys are given. Make absolutely no exceptions to this rule. As you will see later, when I cover the eviction process, a deposit equal to one full month's rent is necessary in order to reduce your losses.

Pro-rating the Rent

If the unit is rented on January 16th, for example, pro-ration of rent is necessary in order to have all your rents due on the first of the month. However, do not pro-rate January's rent. Instead calculate the pro-ration for the February 1st payment, after you have received one full month of rent and the deposit. To illustrate my example:

Jan. 16	$325.00 deposit
	$325.00 rent
Feb. 1	$162.50 rent for balance of Feb. 16-30
March 1	$325.00 rent

Let me emphasize this: never pro-rate rent at the time of move-in. Get the full month's rent and deposit up-front. In my example above, the lease would officially begin on February 1st, and all subsequent rents would be due on the first as well. Remember, welfare checks come out on the first of the month, so all rents should be due then also.

The Rental Application

An application must always be filled out as extensively as possible. Assume that every renter is a debtor-to-be. The information you gather now will be needed by a collection agency to locate and collect any money owed to you. So always verify the name and social security number by checking a driver's license or other supporting identification.

The Rental Agreement

Obtain a standard lease from an office supply store or from a collection agency that specializes in rent collections. A standard lease in which you can incorporate a 10 percent late fee is best.

Sign only a month-to-month lease. This makes it easier to get rid of undesirable tenants who do pay rent. If tenants are filthy, using drugs, or are destructive to the property, you are not shackled to the balance of a year-long lease. All you must do is simply give a 30-day written notice for the tenant to vacate, specifying that you are terminating the month-to-month lease. An explanation is neither necessary nor required.

Only one person should sign as lessee if the tenants are unmarried, even if two divorced women with children apply. Discuss who is to take the responsibility for renting the apartment and who will move out first. Your tenant should be the person who is employed or is receiving the welfare check, not the live-in friend without a job. There are three reasons for this. First, it is easier to evict just one person. Finding and locating two people to serve court notices to could cause a delay in the eviction process. Secondly, if your tenant gets behind on the rent, the welfare agencies will be more apt to help. Usually there is no argument about who will sign, since those on welfare are not allowed to have anyone else living there anyway. If they see a second name on the lease, perhaps no help will be given. Lastly, the welfare recipient is usually the more permanent tenant. The check will come to this address and the children will be registered in a school nearby. The parent must provide adequate housing for them to continue the assistance. The welfare parent cannot just pick up and move tonight. When your renter and the live-in friend split up, the friend will move out and your renter will stay. With this scenario, your lease remains intact.

Be careful about signing a live-in friend as a guarantor on the lease. If he or she does not have a job or earns a low hourly income, there is no point. With the friend's name on the lease as guarantor, you are creating a situation where you have another person to name in the eviction. This is more of a hassle to you than a threat to the renter. Once the bailiff serves one person, he will rarely serve papers to the other. The Columbus bailiffs recognize and avoid this problem by serving one person both eviction court papers. You may not be so lucky in your city.

Incidentally, at least every other month, I get a call from a tenant who informs me that the live-in friend moved out. The tenant would like the locks changed and a new lease drawn up. Of course, my reply is, "The friend's not on the lease."

Utilize a post office box for all of your business dealings, leases included. This eliminates more problems than I care to imagine. Make sure that the tenants not know where you live.

A Word About the Utilities

Do not permit new tenants to move in before the gas meter has been read. You'll find tenants who will run the thermostat up to 95 degrees and then not let the gas company in to read the meter or do a gas line check. This is particularly a problem when the meter is inside. Once it took me three weeks to get the meter read. I was "burned" again!

When you have a vacancy, the best way to handle the utilities is to have the gas turned off but the electricity left on in the wintertime. If you are in a cold climate, put an electric space heater in the basement and point it toward the water meter and hot water tank. Turn the water off in that unit. Open the washing machine faucets in the basement and all the faucets upstairs to drain the water lines. Flush the toilet to empty the tank. Put antifreeze in both the toilet bowl and toilet tank. This takes care of two potential problems. First, you won't worry about getting the meter read and secondly, you won't be paying to heat a vacant unit. This works on typical move-outs where minimal repairs are being completed. However if a new kitchen floor or major drywall patching has been done recently, this won't apply. You must allow adequate time for tile glue and drywall compound to set up in a warm room. In this case, leave the heat on low and be sure to have the meter actually read before giving out keys.

Rent-a-Cop

Once you've acquired many units, rent collection becomes time-consuming. I insist on cash or money orders from my tenants, as I don't accept checks. But carrying that much cash sets you up as easy prey. As a safeguard, I call the city police department special duty unit and hire a uniformed, armed guard at $24 per hour. He collects rents with me from 5 to 8 pm on the first and second of each month. I'm safe and the cost is tax-deductible!

The Best Benefit of All

In this chapter, you've read about the precautions I routinely take to insure that my investment will be profitable and secure. Some of these are precautions that I may not have had to take in neighborhoods where the average renter has an excellent credit history. Sure, I do work a little harder to keep good renters and maintain my property, but would I prefer to own buildings only in upscale areas? Not at all. Problems with renters can occur anywhere. As I've discussed, there are definite financial benefits from investments in lower-income neighborhoods. But the best benefit of all is the satisfaction I have in improving the community and in providing clean, attractive homes for renters who may never have had the opportunity of living in pleasant surroundings. In the next chapter, you'll learn how to nip problems in the bud and deal with difficult renters.

SAMPLE RENTAL APPLICATION

RENTAL APPLICATION

Property Location _____ Apt # _____ Date _____

Number of Bedrooms _____ Maximum Number of Occupants _____ Date Available _____

CONDITIONS OF OCCUPANCY

Lease Term _____ Monthly Rent $ _____ Security Deposit $ _____

Date Rent Begins _____ Prorated Rent $ _____ Pet Fee $ _____

Utilities Paid By Renter: Gas ___ Elec. ___ Water ___ Sewer ___ Other _____

Pets: No ___ Yes ___ Limitations _____ Unfurnished ___ Furnished ___ Range ___ Dishwasher ___ Refrigerator ___

TO BE COMPLETED BY APPLICANT

APPLICANT'S NAME _____ _____ _____
              Last   First   Middle Initial

Date of Birth _____ Soc. Sec. # _____ **Marital Status** ___ Married ___ Single ___ Widowed ___ Separated ___ Divorced

Present Address _____ _____ _____ _____ Phone # ( ) _____
           Street   City   State   Zip Code

Present Owner _____ Owner's Phone # ( ) _____

Owner's Address _____ _____ _____ Rent Amt. $ _____ Length of Occupancy _____
           Street   City   State   Zip Code

Previous Address _____ _____ _____ _____
           Street   City   State   Zip Code

Previous Owner _____ Owner's Phone # ( ) _____

Owner's Address _____ _____ _____ Rent Amt. $ _____ Length of Occupancy _____
           Street   City   State   Zip Code

This form used with permission of Federal Adjustment Bureau, Inc.
1160 Goodale Blvd., Columbus, Ohio 43212

Applicant's
Present Employer _____ Supervisor _____

Employer's Address _____
Street   City   State   Zip Code

Position _____ Dept. # _____ Telephone # (___) _____ Ext. # _____
     Fulltime _____

Present Monthly Income (gross) $ _____ Length of Employment _____ Parttime _____

Previous Employer _____ Supervisor _____

Address _____
Street   City   State   Zip Code

Position _____ Dept. # _____ Telephone # (___) _____
     Fulltime _____

Previous Monthly Income (gross) $ _____ Length of Employment _____ Parttime _____

SPOUSE NAME _____ Maiden Name _____

Date of
Birth _____ Social Security # _____

Spouse's
Present Employer _____ Supervisor _____

Employer's Address _____
Street   City   State   Zip Code

Position _____ Dept. # _____ Telephone # (___) _____
     Fulltime _____

Present Monthly Income (gross) $ _____ Length of Employment _____ Parttime _____

Spouse's
Previous Employer _____ Supervisor _____

Address _____
Street   City   State   Zip Code

Position _____ Dept. # _____ Telephone # (___) _____
     Fulltime _____

Previous Monthly Income (gross) $ _____ Length of Employment _____ Parttime _____

SAMPLE RENTAL APPLICATION (side 2)

VEHICLES

(1) Year _____ Make _____ Model _____ License # _____

(2) Year _____ Make _____ Model _____ License # _____

CREDIT CARDS

Name _____ Name _____

Name _____ Name _____

BANK REFERENCES

Bank Name _____ Checking Acct. # _____

Bank Name _____ Savings Acct. # _____

PERSONAL REFERENCES

Name _____ Telephone No. ( ) _____

Address _____ Street _____ City _____ State _____ Zip Code _____

Name _____ Telephone No. ( ) _____

Address _____ Street _____ City _____ State _____ Zip Code _____

TRADE REFERENCES

Name _____ Telephone No. ( ) _____

Address _____ Street _____ City _____ State _____ Zip Code _____

Name _____ Telephone No. ( ) _____

Address _____ Street _____ City _____ State _____ Zip Code _____

EMERGENCY

(List relative or friend)

Name _____ Relationship _____ Telephone No. ( ) _____

Address _____ Street _____ City _____ State _____ Zip Code _____

Name _____ Relationship _____ Telephone No. ( )_____

Address _____
　　　　　Street　　　　　　　　　　　　　　　City

I hereby deposit with owner/agent, the sum of $ _____ as _____ partial _____ full security deposit on the above premises pending execution of a lease agreement. I understand that my deposit may be applied toward any rent loss, advertising costs, re-rental fees, etc., if this application is approved and I am unable to fulfill the conditions of the lease agreement. The deposit will be returned if this application is not approved, providing all the above questions are answered correctly and truthfully.

I hereby grant permission to the owner/agent to verify through Federal Adjustment Bureau, Inc., the validity of all the above statements to be true and correct. I understand that this application does not constitute any oral and/or written commitments on the part of the owner/agent.

A payment of $ _____ is included herewith, which payment is made for the purpose of verifying the information included on this application. I understand this charge is not under any circumstances, to be returned to me.

_____ _____
Applicant　　　　　　　　　　　　　　　　　　　　　Date

_____ _____
Applicant　　　　　　　　　　　　　　　　　　　　　Date

Please list any additional occupants that will occupy premises (not including roommates)

_____ Relationship _____ Age _____

_____ Relationship _____ Age _____

_____ Relationship _____ Age _____

Application Taken By: _____ Date _____ Fee Rec'd $ _____

Application: Approved _____ Rejected _____ Date Applicant Notified _____

SAMPLE RENTAL AGREEMENT

Rental Agreement

READ CAREFULLY, THIS IS A LEGAL AND BINDING CONTRACT

This Rental Agreement, made this __16__ day of __JANUARY__, 19 __94__, by and between __H. ROGER NEAL__ the owner of the premises, described below, said owner being here-inafter referred to as "Owner," through its agent __H. ROGER NEAL__ hereinafter referred to as "Agent;" and __JOHN R. DOE__ hereinafter referred to as "Resident."

WITNESSETH, that Owner, in consideration of the rent to be paid and the covenants and agreements to be performed by Resident, does hereby rent the following described premises, to wit: Situated in the City of __COLUMBUS__, County of __FRANKLIN__ and State of __OHIO__, known as __0000 CLEVELAND AVE. COLUMBUS, OH 43211__.

TERM AND PAYMENTS

Resident agrees to occupy said premises for an Original term of __ONE MONTH__ said term to commence on the __FEB. 1__, 19 __94__, and agrees to pay without demand the rental of $ __350.00__ on or before the 1st of each and every month beginning on payable on equal monthly installments of $ __350.__. Any and all payments to be paid by the Resident under this agreement are to be __FEBRUARY__ 1st, 19 __94__. Any and all payments to be paid by the Resident under this agreement are to be paid to __H. ROGER NEAL__ at __P.O. BOX 000, COLUMBUS, OH 00000 (MY PHONE #)__, or such other place as shall be designated by __H. ROGER NEAL__.

All payments are to be made in cash, certified check, or money orders or other method approved by the Owner or Agent.

LATE CHARGE

In the event Resident pays any monthly installment after the __2__ day of the month, there will be a late charge of $ __35.__ per day with a maximum charge of __10% of monthly balance due.__.

1. **ACCELERATION.** If Resident fails to pay any installment of rent when same becomes due and payable, the entire amount due under this agreement shall at once become due and payable.

This form used with permission of Federal Adjustment Bureau, Inc.
1160 Goodale Blvd., Columbus, Ohio 43212

2. **SECURITY DEPOSIT.** Resident has deposited with the Owner or Agent a Security Deposit in the amount of $ **350.⁰⁰**. Said Security Deposit is to guarantee the return of the premises to the Owner in the same or better condition as when accepted by the Resident, reasonable wear excepted. The Security Deposit is to indemnify Owner against damage and/or loss of value as a result of Resident's action, mistake, or inaction during the term of occupancy. The Security Deposit may not be applied by the Resident as and for payment of any rent due the Owner prior to the vacation of the premises by the Resident. Should the Resident be responsible for damage and/or loss of value to the premises greater than the value of the Security Deposit, Resident agrees to reimburse the Owner for such loss immediately upon presentation of a bill for said damage and/or loss.

3. **NOTICE TO TERMINATE AND RENEWAL.** Unless another rental agreement is signed by the parties hereto or unless written notice of termination is given by one party to the other thirty (30) days before expiration of this agreement, this contract shall be automatically renewed on a month-to-month basis and may be terminated thereafter by either party upon the giving of written notice to the other party thirty (30) days prior to the next periodic rental due date. Resident shall include with said notice a forwarding address if one is available. Termination shall take place only on the last day of any given month unless otherwise agreed to in writing.

Upon vacating Resident agrees to return the premises to the Owner in the same or better condition as when received, reasonable wear excepted. Under no circumstances shall a dirty or broken condition of the premises, appliances or fixtures be considered to have resulted from reasonable wear.

4. **EXAMINATION OF PREMISES.** Resident has examined the premises and has accepted same as habitable and satisfactory. Resident shall have 72 hours after entering the premises in which to examine same for defects or damages and report said findings to the Owner or Owner's Agent. Resident while residing in said premises shall observe and act in accordance with all Rules and Regulations attached hereto and made a part hereof as if fully rewritten herein.

5. **RESIDENT'S RESPONSIBILITY. The Resident Shall:**

   1) KEEP THAT PART OF THE PREMISES THAT HE OCCUPIES AND USES SAFE AND SANITARY;

   2) DISPOSE OF ALL RUBBISH, GARBAGE, AND OTHER WASTE IN A CLEAN, SAFE, AND SANITARY MANNER;

   3) KEEP ALL PLUMBING FIXTURES IN THE DWELLING UNIT OR USED BY RESIDENT AS CLEAN AS THEIR CONDITION PERMITS;

   4) USE AND OPERATE ALL ELECTRICAL AND PLUMBING FIXTURES PROPERLY;

   5) COMPLY WITH THE REQUIREMENTS IMPOSED ON RESIDENTS BY ALL APPLICABLE STATE AND LOCAL HOUSING, HEALTH, AND SAFETY CODES;

   6) PERSONALLY REFRAIN, AND FORBID ANY OTHER PERSON WHO IS ON THE PREMISES WITH HIS PERMISSION, FROM INTENTIONALLY OR NEGLIGENTLY DESTROYING, DEFACING, DAMAGING, OR REMOVING ANY FIXTURE, APPLIANCE OR OTHER PART OF THE PREMISES;

   7) MAINTAIN IN GOOD WORKING ORDER AND CONDITION ANY RANGE, REFRIGERATOR, WASHER, DRYER, DISHWASHER, OR OTHER APPLIANCES SUPPLIED BY THE OWNER AND REQUIRED TO BE MAINTAINED BY THE RESIDENT UNDER THE TERMS AND CONDITIONS OF THIS RENTAL AGREEMENT;

   8) CONDUCT HIMSELF AND REQUIRE OTHER PERSONS ON THE PREMISES WITH HIS CONSENT TO CONDUCT THEMSELVES IN A MANNER THAT WILL NOT DISTURB HIS NEIGHBORS' PEACEFUL ENJOYMENT OF THE PREMISES.

   9) THE RESIDENT SHALL NOT UNREASONABLY WITHHOLD CONSENT FOR THE OWNER TO ENTER ON THE PREMISES IN ORDER TO INSPECT SAID PREMISES, MAKE ORDINARY, NECESSARY, OR AGREED REPAIRS, DECORATIONS, ALTERATIONS, OR IMPROVEMENTS, DELIVER PARCELS WHICH ARE TOO LARGE FOR THE RESIDENT'S MAIL FACILITIES, SUPPLY NECESSARY OR AGREED SERVICES, OR EXHIBIT THE PREMISES TO PROSPECTIVE OR ACTUAL PURCHASERS, MORTGAGES, OTHER RESIDENTS, WORKMEN OR CONTRACTORS.

FAB 1200 L
Rev. 4/88

SAMPLE RENTAL AGREEMENT (side 2)

6. **OWNER'S RESPONSIBILITY. The Owner Shall:**

   1) COMPLY WITH THE REQUIREMENTS OF ALL APPLICABLE BUILDING, HOUSING, HEALTH, AND SAFETY CODES WHICH MATERIALLY AFFECT HEALTH AND SAFETY;

   2) MAKE ALL REPAIRS AND DO WHATEVER IS REASONABLY NECESSARY TO PUT AND KEEP THE PREMISES IN A FIT AND HABITABLE CONDITION;

   3) KEEP ALL COMMON AREAS OF THE PREMISES IN A SAFE AND SANITARY CONDITION;

   4) MAINTAIN IN GOOD AND SAFE WORKING ORDER AND CONDITION ALL ELECTRICAL, PLUMBING, SANITARY, HEATING, VENTILATING, AND AIR CONDITIONING FIXTURES AND APPLIANCES, AND ELEVATORS, SUPPLIED OR REQUIRED TO BE SUPPLIED;

   5) WHEN HE IS A PARTY TO ANY RENTAL AGREEMENTS THAT COVER FOUR OR MORE DWELLING UNITS IN THE SAME STRUCTURE, PROVIDE AND MAINTAIN APPROPRIATE RECEPTACLES FOR THE REMOVAL OF ASHES, GARBAGE, RUBBISH, AND OTHER WASTE INCIDENTAL TO THE OCCUPANCY OF THE DWELLING UNIT, AND ARRANGE FOR THEIR REMOVAL;

   6) SUPPLY RUNNING WATER, REASONABLE AMOUNTS OF HOT WATER AND REASONABLE HEAT AT ALL TIMES, EXCEPT WHERE THE BUILDING THAT INCLUDES THE PREMISES IS NOT REQUIRED BY LAW TO BE EQUIPPED FOR THAT PURPOSE, OR THE PREMISES IS SO CONSTRUCTED THAT HEAT OR HOT WATER IS GENERATED BY AN INSTALLATION WITHIN THE EXCLUSIVE CONTROL OF THE RESIDENT AND SUPPLIED BY A DIRECT PUBLIC UTILITY CONNECTION;

   7) NOT ABUSE THE RIGHT OF ACCESS CONFERRED BY DIVISION (B) OF SECTION 5321.05 OF THE REVISED CODE;

   8) EXCEPT IN THE CASE OF EMERGENCY OR IF IT IS IMPRACTICABLE TO DO SO, GIVE THE RESIDENT REASONABLE NOTICE OF HIS INTENT TO ENTER AND ENTER ONLY AT REASONABLE TIMES. TWENTY-FOUR HOURS IS PRESUMED TO BE A REASONABLE NOTICE IN THE ABSENCE OF EVIDENCE TO THE CONTRARY.

7. **OWNER'S LIABILITY.** Owner shall not be liable for any damages or losses to person or property caused by anyone not under the direct control and specific order of the Owner. Owner shall not be liable for personal injury or damage or loss of resident's personal property from theft, vandalism, fire, water, rainstorms, smoke, explosions, sonic booms or other causes not within the direct control of the Owner and Resident hereby releases Owner from all liability for such damage. (If protection against loss is desired it is suggested that Resident secure insurance coverage from a reliable company.) Owner shall not be responsible for any damage or injury caused by the failure to keep the premises repaired if the need for said repair was not communicated to the Owner or Owner's Agent by the Resident and was not reasonably within the knowledge of either the Owner or Agent. Owner shall not be liable for damages if Resident is unable to occupy the above premises as of the ___11___ day of ___JANUARY___, 19 __94__ when Resident's inability is due to circumstances not within the control of the Owner or Agent. If the Owner or Agent is not able to deliver possession to the Resident within thirty (30) days of the date set forth above for the commencement of the term, Resident may cancel and terminate this agreement.

8. **UTILITY CHARGES.** Resident agrees to pay all charges and bills incurred for water and sewer, gas, electricity and telephone, which may be assessed or charged against the Resident or Owner for the premises during the term of this Rental Agreement or any continuation thereof except those charges and bills which the Owner has herein agreed to pay.

9. **ALTERATIONS.** Resident agrees not to make any alteration or paint or cover walls or surfaces of the rental premises with any material whatsoever without the prior written consent of the Owner or Agent.

10. **RE-RENTAL CHARGE.** If the Resident vacates the premises prior to fulfillment of this Agreement, additional charges over and above the monthly Rental amount, will be assessed to cover ALL costs incurred by the Owner-Agent in the re-rental of this unit.

11. **EMINENT DOMAIN.** If all or any part of the premises is taken by, or sold under threat of, appropriation, this agreement will terminate as of the date of such taking or sale. The entire award or compensation paid for the property taken or acquired, and for damages to residue, if any, will belong entirely to the Owner and no amount will be payable to the Resident.

12. **PETS.** No pets or animals will be permitted without the prior written consent of the Owner or Agent. Any permission so granted may be revoked at any time by the Owner or Agent.

13. **ASSIGNMENT.** Resident may not assign this Rental Agreement or sublet the premises or any part thereof without the prior written consent of the Owner or Agent.

14. **OCCUPANCY.** Resident agrees that the premises will be used for residential purposes only and will be occupied only by _____
JOHN AND HIS CHILDREN _____ and _____ .

family consisting of _____ persons whose names and ages are _____ .

The premises will not be used or allowed to be used for unlawful or immoral purposes, nor for any purposes deemed hazardous by Owner or Agent or Owner's insurance company because of fire or other risk.

15. **PROPERTY DAMAGE.** In case of partial destruction or injury to the premises by fire, the elements or other casualty not the fault of Owner or Resident, the Owner shall repair the same with reasonable dispatch after notice of such destruction or injury. In the event said premises are rendered totally uninhabitable by fire, the elements or casualty not the fault of the Owner or Resident, or in the event the building of which the above premises are a part (though the premises covered hereunder may not be affected) be so injured or destroyed that the Owner shall decide within a reasonable time not to rebuild, the term of this agreement shall cease and rent shall be due only through the date of such injury or damage.

BREACH OF CONTRACT: In the event lessee(s) is in default of any of the terms or obligations of this Rental Agreement (which includes non-payment of rent, or any rules or regulations herein or hereafter adopted by the lessor for its buildings, its balconies; its courts, its drives, its parking areas or grounds) and lessor requests lessee(s) to vacate the premises as a result thereof or because of said default by lessee(s), lessor initiates a forcible entry and detainer action, by delivering a notice to vacate the premises to lessee(s) as prescribed by Ohio Law, or lessor files a complaint in forcible entry and detainer with the court, or lessor is awarded a judgement order for restitution of the premises, the mere act of vacating the premises by lessee(s) as a result of any of the foregoing acts does not terminate the obligation of the lessee(s) to pay rent for the remainder of the rental period for which no rent has been paid. Lessee(s) remains liable to lessor for all rent and any other damages incurred until the end of the lease term or when the premises are re-rented, whichever ever occurs first.

THIS LEASE SHALL NOT BE BOUND BY ANY TERM, CONDITION, OR REPRESENTATION ORAL OR WRITTEN, NOT SET FORTH HEREIN.

IN WITNESS WHEREOF, Lessor and Lessee have executed this Lease in duplicate on the day and year first written above.

LESSOR _H. Roger Neal_ LESSEE _John A. Doe_

BY _____ LESSEE _____
OWNER - AGENT
OWNER-AGENT/PERSON IN CHARGE

OWNER'S NAME _H. ROGER NEAL_ GUARANTOR _____

ADDRESS _P.O. BOX 000, COLUMBUS, OH_

10

Managing Difficult Tenants

Whenever and wherever you own rental property, you will encounter problem tenants. If you learn how to deal with them quickly and effectively, your investment business will continue on its smooth course, causing little or no disruption to your income and to your business strategy.

Not all tenants are difficult. Some of my tenants have remained in my buildings for up to 21 years. In fact, some of them were here long before I bought the properties. If all tenants were like these, you wouldn't need this chapter full of advice from me. Normal courtesy and common sense would carry you through nicely. But in any rental situation you will sooner or later encounter the hardcore problem tenant who intends to cheat you out of every possible cent. How well you respond to this difficulty will determine how successful your investment business will be.

Up Against the Professionals

It is important to think of problem tenants as professionals in their own right. They've had plenty of experience, they know how far the law will stretch to accommodate their wishes, and they are usually very adept at causing difficulties for the landlord.

When you've owned investment property for awhile, you'll learn how to spot trouble before the rental agreement is signed, but even with experience, you're in for a few surprises from time to time.

Here's an example, from my own units, of a typical hardcore problem tenant and the trouble that can ensue.

Case History: No Money for Rent? No Problem!

Sandi is a single mother on A.D.C., with four children. On occasion, she gets an off-the-record job to supplement her welfare check. She has an appalling credit history and has probably been evicted many times over the years. Soon John, her nonworking adult male friend, moves in and consumes much of Sandi's welfare check. That doesn't bother Sandi, as you might expect it to. If there's no money to pay the rent, she knows that she has a support system to back her up— the welfare agency.

With tenants like Sandi, agencies actually perpetuate the problem. No agency will assist unless the tenant is scheduled for court eviction or utility shut-off, and Sandi knows this. In fact, she knows exactly what her legal rights are, as a tenant. So why pay rent? Why pay utilities? All she must do is take her gas shut-off notice to any one of a number of agencies to get it paid in full. When I start the eviction process and the bailiff tags her door with a 5-day notice, Sandi simply peels off the tag and takes it to an agency for payment. Children's Services comes to her defense and tells me that Sandi just doesn't know how to "prioritize."

Granted, there are handout limitations on the number of times a year that tenants like Sandi can obtain help. One can easily understand and certainly not blame Sandi for using the resources available to her. But she has learned to live on the edge and has lost any moti-

vation to pay rent and meet her obligations. Through their desire to help the impoverished, the agencies have condoned her lack of responsibility.

Tenants like Sandi are plentiful. As a landlord, you must learn to recognize the dangers and realize that once you hand the keys to this type of tenant, you will never see another dime. In this chapter, I hope to convince you of the utmost importance of collecting one full month's rent and one full month's deposit up front.

Tenants Who Won't Pay Rent

The decision not to pay rent is made long before the welfare check arrives in the mail or the paycheck is picked up. Whenever you have a hardcore problem tenant who thinks he or she can outwit you and the system, you are in for trouble. And the tenant is destined for eviction. It is simply a matter of time before both occur.

When you're a landlord, you get used to hearing excuses for nonpayment of rent. In fact, hardcore "nonpays" have their excuses lined up like dominoes. If one doesn't fly, rest assured that another logical reason for the delay awaits you. Here is a list of the excuses most often used on me by tenants whose aim is to avoid paying their rent.

TOP TEN EXCUSES

1. "My check didn't come." (My personal favorite)

2. "My sister has my check."

3. "She is out cashing her check."

4. "Someone stole my check." (Children Services' favorite)

5. "I'm moving." (No boxes are visible)

6. "I cashed my check, and someone stole my money."

7. "I had to pay my gas bill."

8. "My boyfriend got arrested." (Bail or attorney fees)

9. "There was a death in the family, and I had to go out of town." (Expenses)

10. "I don't see why you have to have your rent on the first. Isn't there a grace period?" (Used by only the most arrogant of tenants)

For each excuse listed above, you will find a subsequent list of excuses, lined up and ready to go. As an example of the domino-effect, let's use my personal favorite from above: 1."My check didn't come," and see what follows:

DOMINO EFFECT

1. "My check didn't come."

2. "I will make an appointment with my welfare counselor."

3. "My counselor said that my check will be here in 10-14 days."

4. When the end of the month nears: "There is a double check coming, and I will pay you both months' rent."

5. On the first of the next month: "Only one check came, but I have a job. I will give you one rent now and the balance on payday in two weeks. Come back on the twelfth."

6. Payday never comes. "Welfare found out that I had a job, so I had to quit. But I'm looking for another job." The tenant is, however, willing to make partial payments out of future welfare checks.

7. When you go back on the next month to collect rent and a partial payment, the tenant offers to give you this month's rent, but cannot afford to make payments of any kind toward the amount that is past due. He or she is counting on the fact that now you are in so deep, you'll accept one month's rent and forget about the eviction.

Developing Street Smarts

Now you have come to the realization that you are up against the professional, hardcore, street-smart tenant. There is no limit to what he or she will do to get free rent or piecemeal rent as long as possible. Of course, you will get some good tenants and, at times, some excellent ones, both working people and welfare recipients. But during the rental process it is sometimes difficult to judge how your tenant will act. I've seen those who've been excellent tenants for two years suddenly change their attitude overnight.

Should you be concerned? Should the prospect of difficult tenants deter you from investing in rental housing? No; if you follow the guidelines I've set forth in this book, you will have no trouble in fortifying your inner resources to deal effectively with this problem. If you're dealing with street-smart tenants, you must take the time and make the effort to develop your own "street smarts."

So when faced with the hardcore nonpaying tenant, and the narrative of excuses begins, you must be absolutely firm. You must accept no excuses. When an excuse is given, reply with an eviction notice. Tell the tenant to take the notice to welfare or to another agency right away and get help. Does this sound brutal? The renter is hoping you'll think so! As a landlord, you must learn to recognize the perennial nonpaying tenant immediately. You must act decisively to regain control of the situation and prove that you are not the fool the tenant thought you were.

If you allow the excuses to continue and keep letting the tenants make a fool out of you, someone like me will soon get an excellent buy on your property. Those tenants will surely drive you out of the real estate business completely. In fact, you'll probably be willing to sell your investment for a fraction of what you paid— and you'll finance it as well! (Do you have any other properties that you'd like to sell? I'll be waiting!)

The Reasons Behind the Excuses

Behind every "acceptable" excuse lies a real reason for nonpayment of rent. Tell me what month it is and, in most cases, I'll easily be able to tell you the true reason. Statistically, most nonpays occur in the same months, year-in and year-out:

Worst Months / Real Reasons

April	Easter, spring clothes & gifts
July	July 4th, party weekend
August	State Fair
September	School clothes
December	Christmas gifts and parties

Aside from these fiscal problems I've just listed, you'll find other reasons that are not bound by the calendar: the "new" automobile out back, for example, with a paper license tag showing that it was purchased on rent day. Or the proverbial car up on blocks that is now in good running repair.

Act Immediately

Rent is due on the first of the month. Legally, in Columbus, Ohio, you are permitted to give the eviction notice on the second. Since this timetable varies from state to state, be sure that you study the laws concerning your rights and the rights of your tenants in all matters of rental procedure, including the timing and process of evictions. Your tenants, even the most difficult ones, have rights. The professional troublemakers usually know exactly what these rights are and how to use them to their best advantage. If you are not fully aware of tenants' rights, you will surely violate them, so a copy of your state's landlord/tenant laws is a good investment. You'll find it at a good bookstore or your public library.

When rent is past due, immediate action is absolutely essential. You must stay in control of the situation. While the eviction timetable in your community may vary, this is my customary procedure. If the tenants are not home,

I tape the eviction notice on the front door as soon as the law permits me to do so (on "day two" in my area). The tenants will get the message very quickly that I expect the rent on the first of the month. The eviction notice is actually a 3-day notice to comply (pay the rent) or move out. Officially it is called a Notice to Vacate the Premises and a copy can be purchased at a stationery store that sells legal forms. When I hand it to the tenant or when I tape it to the door and drop by the next day, I'll know immediately whether I'll have an eviction or not. It's very simple: if they pay, they stay. If they do not, I will soon file the eviction.

The 3-day notice covers week days only, meaning Monday through Friday. When you give a timed notice, do not include in your count the day the notice is given, or Saturday and Sunday. As soon as you have notified the tenant and it appears that an eviction will be necessary, prepare the paperwork for the eviction. Get it ready to be filed or to drop off at your attorney's office for filing when the waiting period is up. If I have more that one problem tenant at a time, I give all eviction notices on the second of the month, so that I will have only one court date each month. By making all the evictions on that same day, you'll save yourself several trips downtown. When you own many different properties, time-saving tips like this will make your job easier and more profitable.

Tenants Who Want to Get Even

After you have given the eviction notice, some tenants feel that you have outsmarted them and are determined to get even. A simple phone call by the tenant to the city code enforcement office is all that it takes to harass you. If you have been lax about repairs and maintenance, the code inspector could easily write three full pages of violations on one unit alone, especially after the tenant has had a chance to "work" on the unit. To add to your difficulties, it will be almost impossible to carry out this massive number of repairs while the unit is occupied. Not only do you have a nonpaying tenant who is determined to cause trouble, but you also have the city inspector on your back.

You may encounter other tactics specifically used by tenants to annoy you. They may call the fire department claiming that they "smell carbon monoxide" and want the building declared unsafe. Although firemen know that carbon monoxide is odorless, they will still respond to the call, as they are required to do. And if your heating system is in good repair, as it probably is if you've been conscientious in your upkeep, an inspection will find nothing dangerous. Be prepared for vindictive tenants who spread litter and trash in the alley, then call the Health Department to report filth and roaches. While you may have to clean up the alley yourself and have a professional pest control company exterminate, your tenant's phone calls simply harass and inconvenience you. They can accomplish nothing positive in the tenant's behalf. If you learn to accept annoyances like this and shrug them off, the tenant is the only loser of this game. Now he or she must certainly move.

If there is a bright side to this scenario, it is this: fortunately for you, no phone calls or code violations will stall the eviction process. The tenant will move and you will make the repairs, ready to start the rental process all over again— with the knowledge you've gained from this experience. Problems caused by tenants who want to get even are lessened considerably if you have been conscientiously repairing the unit and seeing that is in excellent condition when vacancies occur. Not only do well-maintained units command higher rents, but they also present fewer difficulties for the landlord.

How to Handle Evictions

There are reasons for managing your real estate investments in a highly protective, systematic, and legal manner as I've emphasized throughout this book. Organization is again apparent when evictions are necessary. Since the eviction process usually takes one month (although this timeline varies in different communities), you will want to have a detailed plan of action for your rental properties, so that the process can be carried out smoothly, amiably (where possible) and with little disruption of your income.

Find Out Where You Stand Now

In order to reduce your losses, it is important that you find out immediately whether or not you are going to collect rent. In low-income neighborhoods, I recommend that you physically collect all the rents. Do not give tenants your self-addressed stamped envelopes. That in itself is proof that you already believe these tenants are incapable of getting stamps and envelopes by themselves. If so, will they then be capable of purchasing money orders and finding mailboxes? I've learned from experience that this method of rent collection simply does not work.

My first eviction was my easiest because I was not led on with excuses or stalling tactics. I remember going up to the unit to introduce myself as the new owner. The tenant received me with some disrespect, stating, "I didn't pay him, and I'm not paying you." I filed for the eviction immediately.

Overcoming Your Fear of Evictions

Some landlords are afraid of evictions. They fear unpleasantness, great monetary losses and even physical reprisal. But the truth of the matter is this: these landlords have not learned that there is a way to evict tenants that clearly changes this picture. So let me set the stage. If you have followed my advice in earlier chapters, the unit is in good condition inside and out, in spite of any superficial damages caused by the tenants.

If the city inspector is called, only minor infractions can be cited because the unit is in excellent repair. You have received one month's full rent as deposit. Although it will take one month for the eviction, if you follow my suggestions, your only monetary loss will be attorney and bailiff fees. Since this is a court procedure, with papers served by the bailiff, the tenant cannot do anything to hurt you. You have written your rental agreement carefully: there is only one lessee to serve court papers to. You do not have to locate the other occupant who comes and goes because he has not signed as lessee.

Many landlords would be surprised to learn that it is possible to maintain good rapport and an open line of communication even through the actual eviction. This makes the process far easier on both parties. To accomplish this, never argue with a tenant. You must always keep the lines of communication open. When you give the first eviction notice to a tenant, be pleasant. Just say, "Nothing personal— I just need the money to pay my bills. I have to make a payment on this building. Take this notice to an agency and line up some help."

Educate Your Tenants

I have always considered it my duty to let the tenants know of these agencies as I hand over the eviction notice. Educate your tenants and discuss their options with them. The first option is this: if the tenants do not move and you do not receive the amount due, you will set their belongings in the front yard after the hearing. By now, you realize that you will definitely not get the rent from the tenant, but the second option solves everyone's problem. With agency assistance, the tenant keeps the apartment, and you get paid. Some tenants believe that such resources are only available to help tenants move, yet many agencies will offer financial help that allows tenants to remain. It is in your interest too, as a landlord, to give your tenant a list of agencies that may be able to provide assistance, such as the welfare department, Children's Services, Volunteers of America, the Salvation Army, the local church your tenant regularly attends, the Y.M.C.A., the Y.W.C.A. and other service organizations I discussed in the previous chapter. These agencies may pay the arrears or assist in referring the tenant to another agency when an additional problem, such as a utility shut-off must be dealt with.

Incidentally, in cold climates, you must make sure that your tenant seeks help immediately in the case of a shut-off notice that will leave the unit unheated. If frozen, the water pipes will do terrible damage. Never have the utilities turned on in your name while a tenant is living in the unit unless you have agreed to provide them, under the terms of your contract, or you'll indeed be "burned again". At best, you can loan electric space heaters for the unit, basement included. However an eviction notice will solve this problem by either ridding you of the tenant, or getting the utilities turned on.

Accept Payment Before the Hearing

Explain that if funds are paid before the court eviction hearing, you will accept them. However, make it clear to the tenant that the total amount due must be paid in full, including not only rent, but also late charges, attorney fees and water bill, plus any court and bailiff fees. Let them know that you will accept this amount at any time before the actual eviction is enforced. However, it is important that you do not delay in filing the eviction, scheduling the hearing, or meeting the bailiff for the set out. While some tenants will go to go to great lengths to stall the legal process, you cannot allow them to remain in the apartment for free. This is a business you are running and you must learn to operate it fairly but also profitably.

Scenario One: How Not to Evict

Throughout my years of investing, my eviction strategy has minimized much of the potential unpleasantness and financial loss. Now let's take a look at what can happen when you, the landlord, choose to evict a tenant without using my method. Here is the scenario: the tenant does not pay the $350 rent on June 1st and decides not to go to an agency for assistance. If you do not file the eviction, you thereby remove the pressure from the tenant. On July 1st, the tenant receives the monthly $483 welfare check. By this time, the two months' rent that you are due totals $700, plus 10 percent late charges and two water bills. In addition, the tenant owes the monthly gas and electric bills, plus other personal bills as well. It doesn't take a graduate from M.I.T. to figure out that you won't receive the total amount due from the tenant's welfare check alone. Maybe it would be a good idea now to give an eviction notice, and encourage the past due tenant to seek help. But, unfortunately, you discover that agencies limit their financial aid. They will offer you a small amount, one that doesn't cover two months' rent. If you don't accept it, the agencies find it cheaper to help the tenant move.

From this point, the tenant will now stay one more month, which is the time it takes for an eviction. (Remember, this timetable may be different in your community.) However, had you acted sooner, the tenant may have been able to stay and the agency would have compensated you for the amount due. Therefore, you hurt both yourself and the tenant by not acting quickly. Providing you have not waited longer to evict, your loss will be two month's rent minus one month's deposit. You have waited exactly one month too long. Of course, there are the legal fees and water bills that I have not taken into account, but, if had you acted sooner, you would have saved yourself one full month's rent of $350 because the deposit would have offset the loss.

Scenario Two: My Eviction Strategy

The timetable for my method goes like this: when the rent is not paid on June 1st, I hand the tenant the eviction notice on June 2nd, which, as I mentioned, is the earliest date permitted in Columbus Ohio. The tenant, who now understands that I will carry through with the eviction, seeks financial assistance. I incur some attorney fees in filing the eviction. By the time the agency helps the tenant, a court date has been set. This is important because agencies will usually not assist without court-served papers. Odds are good that an agency will help the tenant before the court date, which means no additional legal fees and bailiff fees will be charged. All I need is the back rent, a 10 percent late charge, one water bill, and the attorney's filing fees. Once I receive the total amount due, I cancel the eviction. As you've seen, I virtually break even on the process, even if I do have to go to court. Why? Simple arithmetic: it takes one month to evict, and I have one month's deposit.

If eviction laws differ in your area, you will have to adapt my strategy to fit your eviction time schedule. The important point to remember is that you must act quickly. Delay will certainly mean greater financial loss for you and is usually far less beneficial for the tenant.

Many Landlords Are Slow Learners

Who would believe that a landlord could carry out an eviction and still break even? I often speculate about all the sorry-looking landlords I see while sitting in the courtroom. Are any of them going to break even? Would any of them believe that you will? Probably not. In fact while sitting in the hallway before court, I am amazed to hear stories of delinquencies that often involve five months of back rent that will never be recovered. Yet here I am, getting my unit back while still keeping pace with my collections. This technique works so well that I am surprised so few landlords have discovered it.

I only wish that I would be allowed to post a sign at the courtroom where evictions are held, announcing that I buy rental property. I can imagine that so many disillusioned landlords would be trying to reach me that I'd be forced to have sellers take a number!

After the Court Hearing

When the hearing ends, go directly to pay the required fees. You have the option of postponing the bailiff's fee in anticipation that the tenant will move voluntarily. But the time it takes to park and return to the courthouse is not worth the possible savings. Time management is always a consideration for a profitable business.

Beware of stalling tactics sometimes used by tenants who simply don't want to move. For example, as late as two days before the eviction, the tenant may call and ask if there is a dryer hookup in the basement because he or she "will be getting one next week." It may sound convincing. Perhaps the tenant's money difficulties are over. Surely, this wouldn't be a stall tactic would it? I'd bet on it! Although you have already acquired the right to evict the tenants, they may still attempt to draw you into a false sense of security. But it is essential to note that there is a legal maximum time limit allowed from the hearing date to the set out. If the tenant has not been set out by the bailiff within that time limit, the entire eviction process must start all over. Do not allow yourself to be swayed past the deadline by the tenant's stalling tactics.

An Unorthodox Idea: Pay Tenants to Move

Many tenants are clearly reluctant to vacate the unit and this can be a problem for the landlord. But about 12 years ago, I met an investor who shared his technique with me. This man, who was then about 65 years old and who had been in real estate for many years, had a simple method of encouraging tenants to move: he paid them to vacate the unit. At first, I couldn't believe he would even consider such a ridiculous idea. The tenants don't pay rent, and yet I pay them to move? Surely this would mean that the tenant was in command of the situation— or was smarter than I. Shouldn't I be taking control and teaching the tenant a lesson? I remember telling this older investor that I would never pay a tenant to move. Unfortunately, I never saw him again. I would really enjoy telling him now that I have come full circle. Experience has taught me that this is an excellent technique to have in your arsenal.

Once you have proved to the tenant that you are in control, by having court papers served, you are in an excellent position to make a deal. Here's how it works: when the tenant does not pay, I give the eviction notice. I emphasize that it will be filed after the 3-day waiting period and that a $65 attorney fee for filing will be incurred at that time, and a 10% late charge will be added to the amount of rent that is due. At this time, I also discuss agencies that can help. Unfortunately, some tenants do not seek, nor do they want agency assistance. If the tenant has not called within the waiting period, I have the eviction filed. But before I file it, I return to the unit to discuss the eviction status. I inform the tenants that the eviction notice will be filed and that it will only be a matter of time before I have them removed from my apartment. I emphasize that my main goal is to either receive the rent or get my apartment back, vacant and ready to rent again. So I propose that if the tenants move right away, I will "call it even" by accepting the deposit in lieu of rent, cancelling the late charge and attorney's fee. In return, the tenants need not worry about the collection agency, since I will consider the debt paid in full. Sometimes that is all it takes to get them to move that day. If they refuse, I move to phase two: at this time, I offer them a moving allowance of $100 to $200.

This method works well in a situation like one I encountered recently. The tenant's girlfriend had stolen the rent money, there was no gas on to provide heat and, in fact, the tenant had been staying with his parents until an solution could be found. I discussed the situation with the tenant and his mother. Since there was no heat, the son couldn't return to the unit. The parents had been considering government housing for him, but were concerned that a bad credit report by me would prevent him from qualifying for it. We worked out a mutual agreement, whereby each party was released from the rental agreement. We agreed that the keys would be returned, I would change the locks and anything left in the apartment (the girlfriend's property) would be considered abandoned. They agreed to this initial offer, so no additional financial inducement was needed. If necessary, I would have proposed a $100 moving allowance. We loaded his belongings in my truck and it only took four short trips to carry them to his parents' garage. I changed the locks while they were loading up, and immediately I hung my for-rent sign, returning later to clean up.

Now let's take a look at the financial aspects of this technique. Here is a case where the eviction notice was served and filed, and where I did pay a $100 moving allowance.

Case History: A Little Encouragement

Delia's rental arrangements were originally made for me by an agency. In fact, a representative from that agency met me out at the unit and handed me the first month's rent of $325. Later, when Delia couldn't pay a month's rent, I remembered this and contacted the agency representative to let her know that the eviction had already been filed and Delia would have to move. The caseworker informed me that Delia had been in contact with her, seeking more financial aid. Unfortunately, there was a 12-month waiting period for further assistance, so additional financial aid was refused. The caseworker mentioned that she had notified Children's Services and Delia's children would be placed in foster homes upon eviction. When Delia heard this, she was eager to move and find suitable housing elsewhere, since she knew that eviction was inevitable. However, she said that it would take time to find another place and move. I told her that I would give her $100 if she moved today. I even offered to provide transportation for her to the new location. She conceded that it would be in her best interest to accept my offer, and she immediately made arrangements to move in with a relative.

Without paying her to move, it would have taken me three more weeks to evict her. This would have meant three weeks' rent totalling $243.75, $26 in additional attorney fees, $40 in bailiff fees, and $20 to hire two laborers to set her belongings outside. This adds up to $329.75.

I specified that while Delia still owed the rent, the $100 payment for moving expenses did not have to be repaid. But I would send the balance due to a collection agency. She agreed to it in writing as well. What happened to the deposit? Once an eviction has been filed, the tenants know that they will not be receiving their deposits back. Any money that they receive at this point is gravy, so the $100 payment is welcome.

Now, am I really out $100, or am I ahead? Obviously, I am far ahead. Even if I do not rent the unit out until next month, I do not have the $86 in additional expenses. I can advertise the unit and make it available anytime for showings to prospective tenants. Furthermore, I have eliminated a headache and made my job easier and more trouble free. Incidentally, Delia cleaned the unit and returned the keys. Although we agreed that she still had a balance, we parted on good terms. We were both winners in this agreement.

Other Applications of Pay-to-Move

While not all deals are this easy, the Pay-to-Move technique often produces a more amicable parting. Sometimes, though, I have to offer more and accept less: it may take a $200 payment, I may have to give the tenants until Friday at six o'clock to move and I may end up cleaning up the apartment myself. I sometimes even agree to call it even with no collection agency hounding them. But if you take into consideration that you have a deposit, it really does not hurt to give a refund to get rid of a nonpaying tenant.

Positive Ways to Encourage Tenants to Vacate

Here is list, in ascending order, of the inducements I offer to encourage tenants to move:

- Cancel their debt. Reason with them that an eviction will damage their credit and may affect getting future apartments. This logical approach avoids the usual confrontation and you'll both benefit through a parting on good terms. You will get your apartment back immediately and, if the tenants are willing to vacate at once, you'll sign a mutual agreement that precludes a bad credit reference from you.

- Offer a $100 moving allowance without cancelling the debt.

- Offer the $100 moving allowance with debt cancellation.

- Offer a $200 moving allowance with debt cancellation and the right to leave the unit dirty without penalty.

- Purchase furniture and appliances. If you want them to move today and they are moving in with relatives, there may not be enough storage space. You can purchase a nice living room set for $50 and sell it to the new tenant for $50. You can buy their appliances for $100 and sell those for $100. In essence, the idea is not to make money but to facilitate the tenants' immediate move.

When a Set-out Is Necessary

Surprisingly, you can terminate more than half of these problem tenants by using one of these inducements. Unfortunately, there will be those with whom it is impossible to reason. These renters will stay until the evening before, or the morning of, the actual set-out. They want to remain in the unit until the last possible moment. In fact, there are those times when you must actually set all of their belongings into the front yard. Although the deadline is set by the bailiff, somehow they just do not believe it will happen.

When you must do a set-out, bring plenty of helpers and garbage bags. If it is raining or snowing, bring a 10 ft. by 50 ft. roll of plastic to place under and above the items. Since they've been such difficult, unreasonable tenants who certainly deserve to be evicted, you may have looked forward to the prospect of finally being rid of them. But when the time comes, there is no enjoyment whatsoever. There is just the hard reality that someone is now homeless, and the main comfort society will give them is the curb for a pillow.

On the day of the set-out, I discuss with my other nearby tenants how I feel about having to go to court and carrying out an eviction. Any way you look at it, a set-out is an ugly experience, but as a landlord, you certainly cannot be expected to provide for your family and the tenant's family as well. When I do a set-out, I frequently hire my other tenants to help. Not only are they a convenient source of spot labor, but they often can use the additional income. Moreover, they learn a valuable lesson about happens when rent is not paid.

When to Consider Garnishment

If an ex-tenant owes you rent money, you may want to instruct your attorney to begin garnishment proceedings. As a rule of thumb, I consider this option if the person is working full-time and earning $7 an hour or more. When he or she has a lower per-hour wage or no income other than welfare or social security and has no decent car that is fully paid for, garnishment is impractical. There is nothing of value to take or garnish. In such a case, these ex-tenants' debts should be sent to a collection agency, but don't expect to be successful in your efforts to collect. Although I have sent countless tenants to two different agencies over the span of many years, I have received only $25. (When you realize that your chances are slim of ever getting the money after they move, the idea of paying tenants to move immediately sounds more appealing.) Even though you are unlikely to collect the balance due, you should still utilize the collection agency's services. If nothing else, it will serve as a warning flag to other landlords who may consider renting to these tenants in the future.

Removing Tenants When You Buy a Building

I have found that the Pay-to-Move technique can also be put to good use on new acquisitions. When you purchase a property requiring extensive interior repairs that need immediate attention, you can also offer these tenants a moving allowance. Two examples of situations where you may choose to implement this technique are cases of severe code violations and low rents. Granted, all that is needed to raise rents are 30-day notices on month-to-month leases. However, if the units are in dire need of repair, you could hardly increase rents and expect to receive them. With an immediate vacancy, you can start repairs sooner, prevent future problems, and command much higher rents at an earlier date.

Once I acquired a double where the rents were $125 and $175. One side quickly moved and I paid the other tenants a $175 moving allowance for quick removal. They thought I was crazy. They jumped at the offer. I immediately rehabilitated both units and rented the units to Section 8 for $352 and $360 per side, which were good rents in those days.

Druggies And Other Unwanted Tenants

In Ohio and many other states, very strict laws have been passed to encourage landlords to evict tenants who are dealing drugs. However, you are still not legally permitted to evict on the basis of **suspicion** of drug dealing. When I am faced with this situation, for example, I must evict because the tenant is a "neighborhood nuisance" or some similar reason. It is an interesting fact that while I, as a property owner can have my property confiscated for not evicting persons who sell drugs, I may not evict based on my own accusation that they do sell drugs. As a matter if fact, I could no doubt be sued for making such a public accusation. In Ohio, the situation warrants serious consideration. The state can actually take the owner's property away, and in some localities, the city government can board up the building for 12 months. While these laws encourage landlords to keep a close watch on their properties, this has become a serious problem for landlords, especially in the low-income housing districts.

If you feel that you must take steps to protect yourself when you suspect drug activities, call your local police S.W.A.T. Team, document your call and give them a key. (If they go to the unit to "bust" the tenant, they will use the key rather than break down in the door.) However, it generally takes the police months of observation before they act. So odds are that the tenant will be long gone by that time anyway.

If there is visible drug dealing on or near your property, call your local police and provide an address of the location. When a gun is visible and you can give a description of the person, most police departments will act spontaneously. Otherwise, they will work their call into their other police business schedule. This often is effective, however, because the presence of a police car driving by often enough will usually convince the druggies to scatter.

With one of my units, I warned my working tenant that I knew of the drug-dealing that was taking place there while she was at work, and would call the police if I saw further evidence of it. When it reoccurred, I called 911 to report that there was a group of men selling drugs, holding wads of money in one hand and sandwich bags of crack in the other. I was specific in my charge that the unit was being used to count and organize the money and drugs. Within 5 minutes there were police cars everywhere and a helicopter as well. They acted quickly, arresting my tenant's son and placing his baby in the hands of Children's Services. The emergency 911 service will respond in drug-dealing cases, but in many communities will not come immediately unless there is a gun involved.

How to Survive a Filthy Tenant

Filthy tenants can be a major problem. Not only will they destroy the apartment inside and leave a littered yard outside, but they will also drive away your good tenants.

Here is how to solve that problem. As you recall, all tenants are renting on a month-to-month basis. You also have a full deposit. On the first of the month, collect the rent and then give a 30-day written notice to vacate to the tenant. Do not stipulate in writing your reason for the notice. Under the terms of your standard rental agreement, you need not express a reason for asking a tenant to move, just as the tenant also does not need to offer you a reason for moving. When you have issued a 30-day notice, keep a copy of it for your records. Inform the tenant that rent will not be accepted next month. If the tenant is still there next month, give an eviction notice on the second of the month (or as soon as it is permitted in your community). By the way, this is an ideal time to try to pay the tenant to move.

Mastering the Techniques Leads to Success

As I mentioned early in this chapter, problem tenants can be found in any and all types of rental housing. Your success as a landlord will depend upon how well you are able to handle the difficulties they present. Experience helps; that's why I hope you will study and absorb the tips and techniques I have shared from my own years in the business. But another factor in the success of your venture will be the underlying organization and planning that goes into your business operation.

In the following chapter, I'll describe how to set up and maintain an efficient home office, how to handle problems on the go, and how to conduct your business so that it offers you both pleasure and profit.

Part VI
The Business
of Investing

11

Setting Up Your Office

When you're starting your investment business, you may decide that all you need is a telephone and a place to stack messages and newspapers. Although this strategy will no doubt get you through, it lacks the planning and foresight you'll need to succeed. When you purchase your first property, you'll find yourself caught up in an intense scramble of business activity. The time to get organized is before you invest. This chapter deals with that organization process and with the large purchases that you will eventually phase into your business for smoother operation.

Since I am always conscious of expense reduction and profit maximization, I prefer to maintain only an office at home. For years I dreamed of a beautiful office in an upscale part of town, with a small staff to shuffle my paperwork and answer my calls. But when I consider expenses, wages, and the impracticality of having an office elsewhere, it is easy for me to squelch this daydream. My goal is to maximize income and convenience, and the office away from home defeats that goal.

A den or spare bedroom makes an ideal home office. However, if you are just beginning, you can get by with a very small area. You may even start your business like I did, with a file cabinet or cardboard file boxes in the dining room. For a while I used the telephone in the kitchen for my business calls. But eventually, you will outgrow this set-up and you'll need to find a larger, enclosed area to function efficiently. Stake your claim to that extra bedroom or to a specially designated area in the basement. Now you're ready for a desk, an answering machine and a few pieces of business equipment. Since I like to make my surroundings as pleasant as possible, I keep a radio in my office, as well as a remote-controlled 13" television hooked up to cable service. I find it quite enjoyable having sporting events playing in the background as I work.

Your Business Lifeline: The Telephone

You may choose to have a completely separate phone line which you reserve solely for business usage, and certainly, if there are several family members using your primary line, a separate line is desirable. Regardless of your decision, make sure that your phone line has three important features: call waiting, three-way calling, and call-forwarding. If you follow my strategy of buying investment properties in a lower-income neighborhood, few of your tenants will have a phone. If tenants or prospective tenants are calling from a pay phone and the line is busy, they may hang up and not retry your number.

The call-forwarding feature comes in handy if no one is at home to receive an important call. Rather than driving all the way home and discovering an important call on the answering machine that takes me back to my investment neighborhood, I simply have my calls forwarded to my truck automatically. A three-way calling feature enables someone at home to screen my calls before sending them on to my mobile phone. These features are offered by most telephone companies at a minimal cost per month.

Once you are actively in business, you will need a phone in your vehicle. The least expensive models and those offering the best reception possible are those that are permanently installed. When shopping, look for a feature that will honk the horn when the phone rings. This way you'll miss very few calls. However, make sure you let prospective callers know that they should allow time for you to return to the vehicle to answer the phone.

The 3-watt vehicle-affixed phone provides excellent reception. However, if you are looking for comfort and convenience, you might consider a hand-held .6 watt mobile telephone, small and portable enough to hang on your belt. This makes an ideal complement to the truck phone. Because of its lower wattage, your reception will not be as good. Another disadvantage is that you must recharge it every night, but you won't miss calls while you're in the hardware store and you won't have to run to answer the phone anymore. By activating the No Answer/Busy Transfer option, you'll be able to forward calls to your belt phone when you are not in your truck.

Your home or home office number should either be unlisted, or at the very least, listed without an address. Your privacy is extremely important. Never, under any circumstances, should you give a tenant your mobile phone number. Nor should you use it on signs or in advertising. Since you're paying by the minute for these calls, you don't want to be bothered by nuisance calls from tenants asking if they can paint the walls. Calls of this type can be dealt with in the evening. Then, too, you may have tenants who are annoyed at you and who will call simply to irritate you. Instruct your tenants to call your home office number immediately in case of emergency. If there is no one at home who can put through a three-way call to your mobile phone, you can call in frequently to get messages from your answering machine or use the call-forwarding option to direct your calls automatically to your mobile phone.

These features are especially useful to me when it is time to collect rent. In this business, the sooner the information is received, the better off you'll be. Many tenants will call when they receive their checks, and ask me to collect the rent. This I do consider an important call!

Excellent telephone service which includes the features and equipment I've mentioned permits you to function on a professional and efficient level, allowing you to practice the proper time management that will play an integral role in your success.

Investing in Business Equipment

Business equipment can be very expensive and only you will know when you can afford to make the purchases. I recommend, however, that the first piece of equipment you buy should be a copy machine. Since you'll be dealing with legal forms, make sure that the machine copies both regular and legal size documents. If you can locate a firm that sells used machines, you may be able to get an excellent deal on a copier, like I did. An office had originally leased my machine, but three years later grew out of it. When I had negotiated my best deal, I convinced the dealer to throw in the ink, paper, and a warranty as well.

When you have purchased investment property, a facsimile (FAX) machine may be in order, when finances permit. This eliminates many trips to the attorney's office, since, for example, you can transmit your eviction information. Real estate agents and escrow closing officers routinely use FAX machines to send and receive information. Not only are local (and some long-distance) transmissions cheaper than sending a letter, they are considerably more time-efficient.

Your Office Away from Home: Your Truck

You may have always wanted an office away from home, but I'll bet you've never pictured it quite like this— in your truck. Not only does it keep your overhead low, but it's a very practical location for an office. As I drive my truck (and, incidentally, watch my wife take the car), I keep in mind that the money I'm saving equals profit.

When it comes to choosing a truck, forget the small, 4-wheel-drive model with the flashy paint job. You'll need to mount tool boxes and ladder racks on it, and by the time you're finished, you'll agree that it would be a sin do that to a pretty truck. Furthermore, after about three months, your truck will look old and beat-up anyway. It'll be dirty, paint splattered and banged up by the ladders and tools. People are surprised to hear that my truck is comparatively new, because of the heavy wear it's had.

Purchase a full sized pick-up with a 4' x 8' bed. Money spent on options like stereo, automatic, and air-conditioning make work more tolerable and sometimes even enjoyable. Remember, this is your office away from home; comfort and convenience will facilitate efficiency.

I find it handy to use Velcro® strips to fasten a plastic file tray to the dashboard above the steering wheel. In this file, I store rent cards and eviction notices, so that I have them with me when I need them.

With a well-equipped truck serving as your mobile office you'll be able to function more efficiently. Receiving calls while you are out in the field will allow you to prioritize your work load. For example, if you are in your truck and receive a call that a furnace or thermostat needs attention, you can tend to that emergency immediately. On the other hand, if that message is retrieved when you get home, you must either go back out or call someone to do it for you. My investment strategy insists that you keep costs down, and one of the best ways of doing that is to try to do repairs yourself before calling an expert. Granted, you employ painters and handymen for low-cost contract work, but when it comes to furnaces and such, professionals charge a hefty fee to make the repairs. Perhaps all you'll need is a thermostat, which you keep in your truck inventory, so why pay top dollar for the thermostat itself and $28 to the expert who attaches it? If you can't make the repair, at least you tried to "problem solve" before you called the expert. After all, time management means saving money, not just time.

Mounting Tool Boxes and Ladder Racks

When your business is well underway, you'll find it convenient to have tool boxes and ladder racks mounted to your truck. These can be purchased from a truck equipment business. (These shops mount entire truck-beds on new trucks for the gas and electric companies as well, so that's how you can tell that you've found the right place.) I recommend that you buy their best tall, top-side-mount, tool boxes and their highest quality ladder rack. They are not inexpensive; together they will cost around $1,500, but should last through five trucks.

In the tool boxes on the passenger side, you will store power tools and miscellaneous hand tools. On the driver's side will be buckets full of plumbing, electric, and miscellaneous inventory. I've found that the five gallon drywall compound buckets are ideal storage bins. Just saw a little off the top and they will fit nicely. Use this entire side to store materials only. When you need to fix a leaky sink, just pull out the appropriate bucket and carry it in with you. If you need outlet covers or window clips, reach for the bucket of electrical parts. Try to stock the buckets with a variety of items, to reduce the number of trips you'll make to the hardware store.

You'll need a total of four ladders. One 16-ft. and two 32-ft. aluminum ladders are needed for exterior roofing and painting. In addition, buy a 6-ft. aluminum ladder for porch and interior repairs. Ladders are rated according to the weight they will support. When you're purchasing one, make sure that it can accommodate a heavy-duty workload; you'll find that it is money well spent when you buy rugged, high-quality equipment.

Outfitting Your Home Office

While careful record-keeping is an essential part of any business, too much unnecessary and unorganized paperwork can certainly impede your success. Here are the forms and documents you'll need to keep on hand, plus my suggestions for organizing the flow of paper.

Once you own property, you'll need a rental application and a blank lease, or rental agreement. These can be obtained from an office supply store or, preferably, from a collection agency that works with rental housing managers. If the documents are not copyrighted material, buy one copy of each, and use a copier to duplicate it inexpensively. If the forms are copyrighted, you are not permitted to copy them. (See pages 140 through 147 for the rental application and rental agreement that I use regularly. However, before you adopt my form, be sure to seek legal advice, since the laws governing leases in your area may be different.)

Purchase a thick three-ring notebook with dividers to use as a leasebook. Buy a three-hole paper punch and punch out all copies of the leases and applications. Now place the copies in the front of the notebook for easy access. Label the dividers with the name of each property you own. In each section, you'll put the completed leases and rental applications for the corresponding units. When a tenant moves or an eviction notice has been given, the lease and application are removed and transferred to a another file, which I'll explain in a moment. The files should be legal-size, 1-1/2" pocket folders. Since they are too wide for many smaller file cabinets, you'll need a legal-size file cabinet or cardboard file boxes to accommodate these longer folders.

When I issue a 3-day notice, the tenant information for that person is moved to the "Eviction" folder, which I keep in my brief case. If the tenant finally does pay, the information is returned to the leasebook. If the tenant moves, still owing money, copies are either sent to my "Attorney" file for garnishment or moved to a "Collection Agency" file, to be dealt with as indicated. If the tenant moves without owing you money, the tenant information is moved to an "ex-tenants" file. Write the year at the top of the file and begin a new file each year.

Organizing Your File Drawers

Use one entire file drawer for property information. Each time you purchase a property, you will leave the closing table with a small stack of papers. In some states, like Ohio, you'll often be handed a thick, heavy abstract, outlining the chain of title for that property. Place the abstract in a legal-size cardboard filing box and store in a safe, dry permanent spot, out of the way of your daily record-keeping. The closing papers and buyer and seller information should be placed in labeled folders containing property information on each of your current holdings. No tenant information should be kept in these files or in this drawer; that is all kept in the lease notebook which you always have with you in a wide brief case. Files of properties that have been sold are transferred to the bottom file drawer.

Designate another file drawer for material purchases. There you'll again keep labeled folders for each property, but in this drawer, the folders house all of the receipts. When you purchase materials, write the property address where the materials will be used on the receipt itself. When you get back to your office, the receipt will be easy to file in the appropriate folder. At year's end, it won't take long to tabulate all of your expenses.

Keeping Track of Rent Payments

Rent cards are needed to keep track of rent payments, but I have never seen any sold that worked well for me. So I went to a printing shop with my specifications and had a thousand of them printed. As you'll see from the one reproduced on page 184, there's room at the top for the tenant's name, address, and phone number. The rent collection information section accommodates the date, notation, rent due, rent paid, and balance due.

Each unit has a corresponding rent card. When a tenant moves, another rent card is stapled to the front of the card for that unit. At year's-end, you may have up to three or four rent cards stapled together for one unit. This system makes it easier at tax time to calculate the rents collected on that unit for the entire year. On January 1st of each year, begin using new rent cards for all of your units, so that each year's rents can be clearly identified for tax purposes. I keep my rent cards in the plastic file tray on the dashboard of my truck, so they are handy to update when a tenant pays his or her rent.

Organizing your Mortgage Payments

As you accumulate properties, you will soon have so many mortgages to pay that it will be difficult to remember them all without careful organization. Here is what I suggest: take a large sheet of accounting paper and list all your mortgages across the top. On the left margin, list the months. When each payment is made, enter the check number in its respective location. This way, you can tell at a glance which payments have been made. You can also enter your large personal payments on this sheet.

Organizing Information by Computer

Software designed especially for property management purposes is available and can make your quarterly or year-end tabulations easy. It varies widely in price and effectiveness, so you'll want to comparison shop carefully before making a commitment to one particular program. Well-stocked software rental shops carry basic bookkeeping programs and sometimes even property management software for you to try out before purchasing. However, since much of this business is, by necessity, conducted on the site, you will still need portable paper records, such as rent cards and applications.

Checking Accounts And Business Credit

Maintain a separate checking account for your business transactions only. If all of your rental properties are owned by you alone, one business checking account will suffice. If some of the properties are owned by a partnership— you and a partner— you'll need a separate account for the business carried out by that partnership. Unless you have incorporated or have a formal partnership or business under an assumed business name (for example: Best-Ever Investment Properties), open up personal accounts and number them Special Accounts I, II, and III.

When you purchase materials for your units, open separate accounts for each business entity. You'll have one account, for instance, for materials used in the buildings you own yourself and a second account for your partnership. With separate accounts, paint and materials can be charged to the respective business entity and paid from the corresponding checking account.

Of course, you'll want to open accounts at a paint store, a plumbing supplies outlet, a lighting fixtures firm and so on. It's a bit of a nuisance to do the paperwork to open an account, but often it's worth the time invested. My lighting fixtures account, for example, gives me a 30-percent discount on items I charge. You can imagine the savings I realize on all of the materials I purchase for my various properties. If you have difficulty establishing credit at first, there surely is one firm that will allow you to open an account. From then on, you can use that firm as your business credit reference.

Establish a Business Code of Conduct

Over the years, I have established a business code of conduct for myself that I would like to share with you.

- Always conduct yourself in your business dealings in an honest manner. Occasionally tenants will ask you to lie to the phone or gas company in order that they will be able to obtain new service and avoid a past due bill. Never lie for them. If the tenants cannot get the gas turned on honestly, they simply must move. Your credibility is important; if the utility company catches you in a lie, it will be years before they believe anything you say. Your truthfulness has a side-benefit too. When you tell the tenants that you will never tell a lie, they learn that they can trust you because they know you're honest.

- Never get into an argument with a tenant. If one occurs, it will very likely close the line of communication. However it is important to always maintain communication, so that rent money can be accepted or you can make arrangements for the tenant to move. At the very least, open communication allows you to know when the tenant is planning to move.

- Never get angry at tenants or take it personally when tenants do not pay rent. Expect your share of nonpays, accept this as a necessary part of your business, and make the best of it.

- Treat all tenants with respect at all times. If you are accustomed to speaking your mind, this will take some adjustment for you, especially during the eviction process. But a courteous approach will surprise and sometimes shock your nonpaying tenants. They expect a nasty attitude, but if you are respectful, they will nearly always respond in kind.

- Treat everyone as your equal. Never act as though you are better than anyone else, whether employees, tenants, merchants or fellow landlords. Learn to say "please" when asking someone to do something, and "thank you" when they do it. After all this is your job; it's up to you to make your workplace a pleasant place to be.

RENT CARD

APT. NO.	DATE DUE	RENT $

Resident _____
Address _____
Home Telephone _____ Work Telephone _____
Employer _____
Date of Lease: from _____ to _____
Remarks _____

ITEM CODES: **LC** - Late Charge   **P** - Payment   **R** - Rent   **SD** - Security Deposit

DATE	MEMO	PERIOD		DUE	PAYMENT	BALANCE
		From	To			

Part VII
Selling and
Exchanging Properties

12

Selling Your Investment Properties

$\mathbf{A}$s you know by now, my investment strategy encourages you to purchase and maintain a portfolio of rental properties. I recommend that you buy most properties with the intention of holding on to them, rather than turning them over quickly. There are times, however, when it is in your best interest to sell. This chapter will help you identify those times and profit from them.

In the real estate investment business, there are two caveats that are worth noting. Here is the first: don't fall in love with your real estate. You can love the real estate business as a whole, but don't become attached to individual properties. Any kind of emotional involvement will retard your progress and affect your judgment. You'll make poor decisions, which are very likely to cause a reduction in your cash flow. For example, you may opt for exorbitant and unnecessary repairs. Then, too, your attachment to your property may prevent you from selling at a most opportune time.

The second caveat is this: don't believe for a second that you will benefit from an increase in property values. Many properties similar to those I bought a decade ago for $16,000 can be bought for that same price even today. Even in a real estate market like ours in Columbus, Ohio, where housing prices in general have been rising, I cannot count on inflation to boost the prices of my investment properties. That is why my emphasis is always on cash flow and income, rather than on increasing my equity by sitting back and waiting until the prices rise.

The way to sell low-income real estate at a profit is to buy at a depressed purchase price. This usually means that the building will be dilapidated as well. So in order for you to sell it for more than you paid, you must make visible repairs and increase rents. This is why you must buy right, as I've described in earlier chapters; you must allow yourself a large margin for selling. If you paid too high a price and are financially buried in your properties, this chapter cannot help bail you out. Instead it is intended for those investors who have been faithfully following my strategy. Unlike other sellers, you will not sell to escape from a greedy investment that is claiming your time, your money and your energy. Your motivation for selling will be a positive one. You'll be selling to facilitate the purchase of more property or perhaps to consolidate your investments.

Cash Out: The Quick Turnover

Occasionally, you may be interested in buying a building with the intention of reselling it quickly, in order to increase your cash reserve or to enter into a seller-financing agreement with the new buyer, for additional income. However, I do not recommend either of these as a full-time endeavor and strategy. If your properties do not turn over quickly, your growth could easily be stagnated. With this in mind, I recommend that you always maintain a portfolio of properties for steady income. Utilize the "buying for selling" strategy as a sideline only.

Whether you're just starting out, or have already acquired several properties, this technique will build or replenish your cash reserve. Let me emphasize, however that the only way this type of transaction will be profitable is if your purchase price was a bargain basement deal. You will require a margin of at least $10,000 to make it worth the risk. After all, when you're cashing out, you may need to enlist the help of a real estate agent or reduce the price to get the property sold. If so, you'll still be left with a net margin of around $5,000.

To accomplish this, you may be tempted to invest in higher-priced properties, where $5,000 or $10,000 is a small percentage of the value— buying a $70,000 building and selling it for $80,000, for example. Don't do it! Buy properties that are in your own specific investment neighborhood, so that if the property does not sell, it won't be a problem. You'll just keep it in your portfolio and you won't be rushed into selling or forced to reduce the price drastically. When buying property for a quick turnover, it is advisable to stay in the low-dollar and low-risk levels. Specifically, invest $20,000 and sell for $30,000. Or even invest $25,000 and sell for $35,000.

Choosing Properties for a Quick Resale

You may have begun to wonder what properties are bought for the sole purpose of reselling. This is not an easy question to answer without sounding contradictory. But there are some rules of thumb to help you in your choice. First of all, never buy a property unless you're willing to keep it indefinitely. The best property for a quick cash-out is one where you have the largest potential margin for profit. Ironically, this is probably the same property which provides the greatest cash flow, and one you'd like to keep in your portfolio. However, if you need more cash for additional purchases, this is the one to put on the market. Don't go to the bank and borrow against it. A big new loan will ruin your investment. Instead, sell it for cash. If you're lucky, you may even bypass the need for a partner on your next property.

Sometimes you'll find that two or three of your properties have high cash profit potential and it's a tough decision choosing which one to sell. In that case, put all three on the market until one has sold. Then withdraw the other one or two and return them to your portfolio. Develop the attitude that whichever property sells first, goes.

Reinvesting the cash from the closing is, as you surely know by now, the best thing for you and your business. After only a couple of deals, you'll be in a position to pay cash for a property, or several properties. You may wish to set aside small amounts of cash to assume loans on properties to add to your portfolio, while the larger balance can be used to buy and sell quick turnover properties. Or you might prefer to try the reverse tactic: use large sums to pay cash for portfolio properties and assume loans with small cash down payments on properties you intend to resell, carrying the financing for the purpose of earning interest on the notes. Either way, your transactions will eventually raise your finances to a level in which you can pay cash for the properties that are to remain in your portfolio. Since your overall goal is to amass twenty doubles and get them all paid off in the shortest period of time, this technique enables you to reach that goal even faster.

An Example of a Profitable Sale

One deal that I am particularly proud of is a property I mentioned briefly earlier in the book. This property was purchased for $13,000 cash. It was a three-bedroom-per-side, frame double that was occupied. When I bought it, the rents were $125 and $175 per side. The double had a new roof but was in dire need of exterior paint, while the interior needed serious cosmetic, heating, and plumbing repairs. This was also back in the days where I provided appliances and storm doors, a practice to which I am now adamantly opposed. The repairs and appliances came to $5,500, bringing my total investment to $18,500. Originally, I rented both sides out to Section 8 renters for $352 and $360 and the tenants paid their own water bills as well. By the time I sold the property, the rents had been increased to $387 per side and the cash flow was superb indeed.

I seized the opportunity to sell the building for $32,500 cash and the closing expenses totalled nearly $2,500. So the check that I received was $30,072.02. Granted, I did have $18,500 cash of my own money in the property, but that still leaves a profit of roughly $11,500. I admit that, overall, this is not a large sum of money. But you will surely agree that this was a hefty return for a small investment amount and a low risk.

It was interesting to watch what happened after the sale. The buyer had big property acquisition plans. He paid cash for the double and his intent was to refinance immediately to get his money back. He figured that he could have the double appraised for $38,000 and borrow 80 percent of the appraised value, or $30,400. With that, he could come close to recouping all of his money and could then buy another double. The property did not appraise for $38,000, but it did appraise, coincidently enough, for $32,000. He was disappointed that his plan was shaken, but he did offer $28,000 cash for another double which I owned. I refused and believed at the time that he would pay much more. Unfortunately, his new tenants quickly put a bad taste in his mouth and he decided to end his real estate venture. Shortly thereafter, I saw a For Sale sign go up in the front yard.

There were two drawbacks to his master plan. One, he worked a fulltime job at a bank and hadn't spent sufficient time doing his homework; he had no idea what he was getting into. Secondly, had his plan worked, he would have ended up with many units but little or no cash flow. His theory sounded so much like my early premise: I truly believed that if I owned enough real estate, I would be rich, when the day came to cash out. Actually, he is very lucky that his plan didn't work immediately and that he lost his enthusiasm before buying other properties and getting deeper in the hole.

On another deal, I found two occupied doubles priced at $15,000 for the pair. The city inspector had cited six pages of violations between the two buildings and the seller was quite thoroughly intimidated. I quickly eliminated the violations and raised the rents. I advertised the buildings for sale and an elderly farmer immediately called to make an appointment for a showing. When he drove up to meet me at the properties, he was driving a late 50's Cadillac. To this day, I remember wondering how he could possibly afford to buy one of the two. Right then and there, however, we wrote an offer to purchase both buildings— for $32,000 cash!

Stay Away From Singles

Do not buy single family homes for resale purposes. First of all, your chances of finding a cash buyer are quite remote. With a single, you'll attract potential buyers who will probably intend to live in it, not investors buying rental property. This advice should never be ignored when you're investing in a low-income neighborhood where many of these homebuyer might have a hard time qualifying for financing. Lenders often have a minimum loan amount that may very well exceed the appraised value of the single. When you have property that investors are interested in, you open up the possibility of finding a cash buyer. (Incidentally, when I refer to a "cash buyer", I am not necessarily talking about someone with the full amount of the purchase price in a checking account at the bank. Perhaps he or she will get a loan secured by other property in order to obtain the cash. Or maybe your buyer has access to favorable financing, through connections with a lending institution.) While not too many of these investors want to pay top dollar for a single family home in a depressed area, I have often seen investors pay sky-high prices for multi-family investment property in low-income neighborhoods.

How Will Your Buyer Pay For the Purchase?

When you sell a property, you'll need to be just as knowledgeable about financing as you are when you're buying. The easiest way to sell a property is by using many of the same methods you considered during your own acquisition, so you may want to review the information covered in Chapter 5. However, I will mention two exceptions to the advice I gave you as a buyer: first, you can feel comfortable, in certain circumstances, selling properties on land contract and second, as a seller, you can accept a balloon payment provision, since you're in control if the buyer defaults. While there may be better ways to structure your sale, selling on land contract and with balloon payments should not let you encounter the pitfalls you would as a buyer.

Let's take a look at the common ways for a buyer to pay for the property you've decided to sell.

Finance Your Sale and Accumulate Notes

As you learned earlier in this book, the properties I choose as investments are difficult to finance with new bank loans. Even after my renovations, the sales price may still be too low to meet the lender's minimum loan amount. So I expect to finance many of the properties I sell; in fact, I look forward to it.

In financing one of my properties— or what I call selling my property on notes— I simply take back first, second, or third mortgages. I agree to accept payment from the buyer, not in a lump sum, but in amortized monthly payments. Just like an institutional lender, I charge interest on the note and make a very nice profit, while encouraging the sale of my property.

The secret ingredient for a successful financing transaction is the knack of finding the right buyers for your property. You need buyers who pay their bills on time and are credit worthy. Perhaps you'll find a buyer who is capable of handling payments on a $10,000 note but not a $40,000 note. Carefully gauge your buyers and do credit checks. Do not judge your buyers by how they dress or by what they drive. Years ago I met a multi-millionaire who drove an old pickup truck and had a hole in his shoe. He told me that he buys "whole streets at a time."

Even if the buyers seem credit worthy, there is no guarantee that they will pay. There is always the possibility that they could overextend themselves at home or with other investments and decide to file bankruptcy. As I mentioned earlier, most investors do not survive in this business. They don't take the time or make an effort to learn survival skills. Your buyers will be no different. The best that you can do is to find the best buyer available who is a good risk, then cross your fingers.

Watch Out for Unscrupulous Buyers

Through the years, I have met many unscrupulous buyers, some with snazzy new cars, who enter into real estate contracts and close deals which they have absolutely no intention of fulfilling. Their down payments are always very small. Their aim is to quickly resell for a larger amount, at which time they too will carry a note. Their aim is to get their down payment back as quickly as possible. If the property doesn't sell, it's bad news for the former owner who's now carrying their note. No payments are ever made. No real estate taxes are ever paid. No water bills are ever paid. No workers or repair expenses are ever paid. If the units are rented, they'll gladly collect rents. If the tenants don't pay, you can bet that these landlords will be the first to file the evictions. I have seen them in court evicting tenants.

Without careful scrutiny of your buyer, you could really be in for an unnerving experience. For these unscrupulous buyers also have an arsenal of attorneys who will take advantage of any loopholes in your contract and mortgage. They operate on the assumption that the prospect of outrageously high attorney fees will prevent you from fighting back. They hope that you'll be content to sit back and wait until they find a buyer. At times they may even produce signed contracts proving to you that someone is interested. There you are, holding the mortgage and hoping that the property eventually will be sold. You think that if you can hold on 'til then, you'll finally be paid. What's your alternative? You're not eager to run up a horrendous legal bill. And to be perfectly truthful, you don't want the property back.

Odds are good that you will never see another dime. As you watch from the sidelines, you can see that no repairs will ever be made and that the building will eventually become uninhabitable. Consider a leaking roof, for example; the interior damage would mount up until the entire building is in ruin.

Case History: An Astonishing Coincidence

I once entered into an agreement on a 6-unit building for $12,000, with the intention of applying for rezoning to an 8-unit, then carrying out a complete rehabilitation. I was in my office discussing this problem in a telephone conversation with the city inspector when a health insurance salesman arrived. I asked him to be seated until I finished my conversation. After a short while, he interrupted my conversation and asked if I was talking about "Mr. So-and-So", the present owner of the property. When I said, "Yes," he announced to my amazement that he held the first mortgage on that property. Coincidences like this so rarely happen that he began to wonder if this was a staged performance. He demanded documentation to verify that I had really been working on the rezoning. He still thought that somehow I was tied in with this unscrupulous character and was trying to set him up for something.

After a while, he loosened up and even began laughing about how this person had swindled him. Here's how it happened: at a closing many years earlier, he took back a first mortgage of $20,000 with very little down. Never again did he receive another dime. When I asked why he hadn't foreclosed, he said that he always thought that someday he would be paid. Eventually the building had deteriorated to the point that the city inspectors condemned it and were trying to have it torn down. Certainly at this point, he did not want the building back. With the deed in his name, he'd have the city on his back. He told me that he would be very willing to take $3,000 and forget the $20,000 balance. He said that he had given up the hope of getting

195

anything years ago anyway and would be grateful to receive even this amount.

Now I began to get excited. I contacted the bank carrying the unscrupulous Mr. So-and-So's second mortgage and found that he had played the same game with them. He got the loan and never paid them a dime either. So even the bank got burned! They had obviously written this off as a bad debt, because it took three weeks for them to even find the loan, which by then had increased to $4,000. We were under a tight deadline, since the city inspector had given me a tear-down date. When I emphasized this to the bank officers, they agreed that they'd be far better off accepting $500 under the circumstances— especially since they had forgotten about the loan.

By then I figured I was ready to close the deal. But when the the title insurance company took a look at the documentation, they refused to close the deal. Apparently this unscrupulous character had used his name on the first deed, but had filed subsequent deeds in different company and individuals' names. This was done to confuse the city inspectors and other creditors, and the title insurance company was just plain scared to touch this deal.

My attorney referred me to a title insurance company that could handle the toughest cases. After plenty of research and a whole host of signatures, the deal finally moved toward closing. While I had the seller gathering and releasing and signing deeds, the closing agent called with the most damaging and final news: the title search had uncovered $51,000 in liens— $17,000 of which were unshakeable I.R.S. encumbrances. The lien amount was far above what I was willing to pay and what the building was worth.

Needless to say, I never did buy the building. In fact, that thief even beat me out of my $100 deposit. When you consider for a moment the total   number of cash deposits that he accepted over the years on purchase offers for this property alone, the magnitude of his crime seems absolutely mind-boggling.

One year after this, the building was torn down. Unfortunately for me, rather than having an 8-unit apartment right next door to my 10-unit, I now have a dirt lot. Although this is a common scam, I know very few of these people. This one in particular is notorious for his misdeeds. It's amazing to me that he is not in jail. If failing to pay your bills is not a crime, in this case it should be. He drives a new van and has fully insulated himself from creditors. Arguably, you could state that he had intent to defraud, but if you're left holding a note, would you pay a lawyer a vast sum of money to try to prove it? Then you may even be sued for defamation of character or for making false accusations. Based on his track record, it's likely he would win.

The Importance of Careful Screening

While this story is, indeed, a nightmare, it should not discourage you from selling your property on notes. However, it should convince you of the importance of careful screening. I have bought and sold more properties than I care to remember. I can attest to the fact that I paid all of my mortgage holders, but like my acquaintance, the health insurance agent, not all have paid me. I have been fortunate, though, that when my buyers have defaulted, I still have managed to recover most of the balance due.

I have suggestions for those of you who are considering selling on notes. To help avoid a scenario similar to the one I related, always run credit checks on your buyers. If you still fall prey to these unscrupulous tactics, foreclose immediately. Treat the buyers with the same scepticism and distrust that you do a tenant who does not pay rent. File the necessary papers as soon as legally possible, because any delay will ultimately make matters worse.

A Profitable Transaction

In spite of the pitfalls with this type of sale, financing your buyer's purchase can be very profitable for you. Let's take, as an example, a double that you bought for $18,000, with $2,000 down and a $16,000 balance on a first mortgage note for 8 years at 9 percent interest. Now you put another $1,500 into cosmetic repairs. Your principal and interest payment is $234.41. Of course you have taxes, insurance, water, and repairs to pay, but only while you own it, so we will not include those specifics. Here is the breakdown:

$16,000	Assumable 1st mortgage
$ 2,000	Down payment
$ 1,500	Improvements
$19,500	Total investment

Now let me walk you through the steps of selling the property by yourself. As we go along, I'll suggest what I would do in this circumstance.

When you're ready to sell, you advertise in the investment section of the Sunday paper. If your building looks good inside and out, if the rental amounts are decent and if you offer financing, the property should sell quickly. Of course, the selling price must be realistic. Suppose you consider an asking price of $30,000, which will allow you plenty of room to come down in the negotiations. For this property, you should require at least a $3,500 down payment. Take back a second mortgage secured by a promissory note with a face value of $5,000 to $10,500 with no balloon payment. The term of the note should be from ten to thirty years, with the interest rate close to or a little higher than the rate an institutional lender might charge (in this case, we'll set the interest rate at 10%). Permit the buyer to assume the first mortgage loan and give the buyer a deed at closing. As an example, if your note is $7,000 for ten years at 10 percent, the payment to you is $92.54 monthly.

This is one of many properties you might sell. Consider what your income would be if you set yourself a secondary goal of collecting ten notes. If you find that the procedure works well for you, you can make the decision to continue the practice. While your primary income will still be derived from your rental units, this offers you another income-producing method to supplement your cash flow income.

Balloons Are Fine if You're a Seller

If you want to be able to obtain large sums of money for future cash deals, you can modify this technique by requiring a balloon payment within one to three years. (Remember: never buy with balloons, but it is acceptable to sell with them.) During the term of the note, you'll receive the income from it, and at the balloon date, you'll receive a lump sum. Resist the temptation to spend it on personal luxuries; these funds should be reinvested in your real estate business. If, once again, you sell and finance ten properties, each with a $7,000 balloon, you'll have a tidy sum for reinvestment.

What happens if your buyer has difficulty paying the balloon when it is due? You and your attorney can always negotiate a "better" note with a higher interest rate and another balloon at a later date.

If the interest rate on your underlying loan assumption is low, it may pay you to sell on Land Contract and wrap the "assumable" loan. This will enable you to profit on the first mortgage as well as on the second. For example, the first mortgage balance is $16,000 at 8 percent interest, you could carry a second mortgage at 11 percent. Or, even better, consider the return if you received 11 percent interest on the total balance of both mortgages. Since you are obligated to pay the first mortgage lender only 8 percent interest, you'd realize a 3 percent profit on the

$16,000 first mortgage as well as the full 11% interest on the remainder. With a land contract, your buyer makes one large payment to you, out of which you will make the first mortgage payment, taxes, and insurance. All the remaining income is profit.

Case History: Regrets, Regrets

Once I spotted a for-sale-by-owner ad in my local paper from an individual who had many properties available. I purchased five doubles from him and he financed all five with down payments ranging from $1,500 to $2,500. In a matter of five months, I sold all five doubles and got my down payments back. My buyers assumed the first mortgage loans and I financed the second mortgages for 30 years with no balloon payments. The five seconds totalled nearly $30,000. When one of my buyers called my seller to introduce himself and to make the first payment on the assumed loan, the seller was angry. He informed the buyer that his payments would be rejected because I was the buyer and therefore was responsible for making the payments. Our attorneys got together and informed his attorney that the payment would be sent anyway because there was nothing in our papers stating that the financing was not assumable. So, in fact, they were able to be assumed.

Although my buyer had excellent credit and a high-paying job, he was a terrible landlord. He was frequently out of town, and his units almost always stood vacant. He called me once and expressed his displeasure, then asked if I would mind if he sold the units. I indicated that this was acceptable to me, but I advised him to take his time and find a good buyer like I did.

He later called again to tell me that he had found a buyer and, coincidentally, one who apparently knew me. When he mentioned the name, I expressed my disappointment with his selection. I knew that this buyer had used similar tactics to the thief whom I spoke of earlier. I expressed fear of losing my investment and going bankrupt. He replied that by that time we would have safe deposit boxes full of money and that it would not matter. I knew we were heading for trouble.

My buyer insisted that I was just making this up and that I was just as recalcitrant as my own seller, the man who had refused to accept the assumption. He emphasized that I just wanted him on the hook because he made his payments. Of course, I was reminded that, like the previous seller, I had to accept the new buyer's payment because our documents did not include a "nonassumable" clause. This is one instance where I regret not including such a clause in an agreement.

Fortunately, my notes did contain a 30-day acceleration clause. This meant that if the new buyer were a month late, I could foreclose if I wanted to.

It took only a couple of months for this to happen. He was not paying me or my seller on his first mortgages. I began foreclosure proceedings immediately on the person to whom I had sold the property. My seller named me, my buyer, and his buyer in his foreclosure. When I contacted the current owner and asked him to just relinquish the units, he refused. He said that he would be stupid to do so and boasted that he could collect lots of rent for months and not pay any bills, which he did. Shortly after the foreclosures, he filed bankruptcy. This was certainly no surprise.

After the foreclosure, I still was on the hook for the first mortgages and my buyer was still on the hook for both the first and second mortgages. Granted, the third buyer was on the hook for the first, second, and third mortgages. But he had no intention of paying anybody. Remember, I had a good buyer. However, he now had problems, the biggest one of which was selling to a deadbeat. But in the final analysis, he lived up to both my initial scrutiny and expectations. He paid the first mortgages to my seller and second mortgages to me. The third mortgages that he held for his buyer were not worth the paper they were written on. My only regret was that I did not make the notes nonassumable. This way his buyer would have cashed me out at the closing or the closing would have not taken place.

Quality Notes Are Worth Their Weight in Gold

To summarize, do not just acquire notes. Acquire good quality notes. In fact, there are many companies that pay cash for notes, paying approximately 80 percent of the balance due. The hitch is that you must have a buyer with a good credit rating. So whether you decide to keep or sell your notes, they are only as good as your buyer. If your buyers are of high caliber, your profit potential is enormous.

I suggest that, in addition to your portfolio of rental units, you hold approximately ten notes at any one time. These may include notes with balloon payments and others with 15- to 30-year term payouts. This provides the assortment that will enhance your financial position, and the balloon payments offer cash boosts. The longevity of the notes extends your income and keeps the payoff low. In other words, if you have a 30-year loan, the payoff in five years is nearly the original loan amount. Had the payout been over an eight-year period, the payoff in five years would be very minimal. I do not recommend selling the quality notes that you have acquired. Giving up 20 percent is losing profit. I prefer to maintain what I have established and maximize my income. If you need cash, get it on the next deal. Secure a balloon payment or sell a property for cash instead of a long-term note. By planning your strategy, you'll find that a portfolio of notes will provide both cash accumulation and monthly income.

Now, consider this: imagine owning twenty free-and-clear doubles and carrying ten notes. My largest note is $76,000, and the smallest is $8,500. While some have balloons, most do not. I prefer long-term notes, but enjoy collecting all varieties. While this technique will not take the place of my original investment strategy, notes will most assuredly continue to supplement my income for many years.

1031 Exchanges: An Alternative to Selling

Currently, buyers and sellers can defer paying the income tax on the capital gains from investment real estate by engaging in a 1031 exchange, rather than selling the property outright. This is an option to consider, especially if consolidation rather than cash is your primary objective. If you own a building that doesn't fit in with your investment plans— perhaps one that is outside your target neighborhood— a 1031 exchange can give you an opportunity to trade that property for one that better serves your needs. The IRS rules for 1031 exchanges are stringent, and I'll cover the basics in the next chapter, when we take a look at the tax considerations that affect investment property.

13

Tax Advantages for Investors

Regardless of which political party holds office, the government has historically smiled favorably on those who invest in real estate. In recent years, we have experienced a few set-backs. Nevertheless, the future of the type of real estate investment I have described in this book is still bright. In this chapter, I will outline three specific tax advantages that are available to you as an investor: depreciation, deferred-tax exchanges and tax credits on investment properties.

The Effect of Recent Tax Laws

When the 1986 Tax Reform Act and subsequent tax rules went into effect, investors were faced with depreciation and loss limitations that sent many of them running scared. Many investors bailed out of real estate altogether for fear they would suffer substantial losses that couldn't be used to offset other income. I remember encountering a frantic seller who wanted to dump fourteen condominiums for $51,500 apiece, when he had recently paid $65,000 for each unit. He was even willing to throw in a $10,000 cash bonus if a buyer would purchase all fourteen units. (I didn't buy them because what I pay for my properties is roughly $10,000 per unit—then and now— and, bargain or not, I couldn't justify buying anything that wouldn't give me an excellent return.)

This example simply illustrates how scared investors were when the tax law changes went into effect. The image of real estate as a profitable investment was certainly tarnished. Even those who were not in real estate at the time were convinced that Congress had effectively put an end to investment profits. In fact, someone recently asked me if investors were still allowed to write off rental mortgage interest; he was indeed surprised when I answered "Yes."

Since I am in real estate for the long haul, depreciating properties over 27.5 years versus 15 to 19 years makes little difference to me. By the same token, the current annual passive loss limitation of $25,000 does not affect me either, for two reasons. First, the limitation does not affect me since I work at my investment business on a full-time basis. Effective after December 31, 1993, the Revenue Reconciliation Act of 1993 has exempted individuals whose "personal services" in the real estate business occupy more than 50% of their time. To qualify for the exemption, they must also "materially participate" in the business, and I certainly do that.

Secondly, I am in this business to make money, not lose it. Granted, there have been many years when I've experienced losses totalling over $25,000 on my rehabilitated and newly-acquired properties alone, but that total was then subtracted from my overall rental income to determine my Total Rental Real Estate Income. The loss limitation affects only those who have losses that exceed their rental income by more than $25,000. Since you, I hope, are planning to make money with your investments, not simply use them as a tax write-off, these tax law changes should not be a problem to you.

Seek Professional Advice

I am neither an accountant, nor a tax attorney; as you know, I am writing from the viewpoint of an investor. But even though I make a point of studying the tax laws and understanding how they will affect my business, I cannot begin to know all of the finer points of law and accounting. That's why I rely on a team of experts to give me specific direction on these matters. I recommend that you consult with a tax attorney and accountant before you invest, and continue that close working relationship as you add to your portfolio or buy properties for quick resale. Don't wait until you've made your move before you ask for advice; many tax advantages are available only to those who plan for them. If you misjudge a time limit, for example, you may find yourself liable for thousands of dollars in taxes that could have been deferred. Let this be your guideline: Make lots of money, then shelter it wisely.

Understanding Depreciation

With the investment strategy I have outlined in this book, the number of years over which you depreciate properties is not important. I consider any depreciation a feature and benefit of investing, rather than a reason to invest.

To be realistic, depreciation on one or two properties in this price range doesn't amount to much anyway. Even if you are tabulating depreciation on twenty such properties, the figure is still comparatively small. (But of course we'll take it anyway!) As an example, let's take a look at the tax basis of $20,000 and $40,000 properties, where the depreciable annual deductions are only $727.27 and $1454.55 respectively. For this example, I have used state and local tax percentages from my own investment area. Your figures are likely to vary at these levels.

Depreciation: 27.5 Years

Tax Basis:		$20,000	$40,000
Federal	28%	$ 203.64	$ 407.28
Ohio	5.2%	$ 37.82	$ 75.64
City	2%	$ 14.55	$ 29.10
Annual tax savings:		$ 256.01	$ 512.02
x 20 properties:		$5,120.20	$10,240.40

Think of depreciation as a "paper expense" that you deduct but do not really spend. In fact, when calculating income for the year, you must add this amount to your taxable income for your true income total. For example, if your taxable income is $100,000 and depreciation is $30,000, then your true income is $130,000.

I've never been particularly impressed with the tax advantages of depreciation. If you depreciate for 5 or even 27.5 years and then sell, you must add all that depreciation to your profit total, thus possibly elevating you to a new, higher income tax bracket. You may end up paying more in taxes than you would have if you had depreciated on a lower annual basis. However, there is one way out of this predicament and this can be a definite tax advantage: the tax-deferred exchange, which I'll discuss in a moment.

The Tax on All That Capital Gain

The tax on capital gains has a direct impact on how I conduct business. If I were to sell and receive a large cash sum at closing, the income taxes could easily eat up my profit. Consider this example: you paid $17,000 for a property and made $3,000 in repairs. That means, you now have $20,000 invested into the property. The $3000 in repairs can be written off or depreciated. Let's assume that you have depreciated another $3,000 for the building itself, and this must be subtracted from your $17,000. Your basis is now $14,000 and everything above that is profit. So if you sell for $30,000, your taxable income is $16,000. If, for example, you pay 28% in federal income tax, 5.2% in state and 2% percent in city taxes, your total tax bill would be a whopping 35.2% of your profit, or $5,632. So instead of leaving the closing table with $13,000 additional cash ($10,000 of it profit), you would have a mere $7,368.

Congress frequently toys with the idea of changing the rules on capital gains tax, but no matter how the laws are written and the calculations made, I do not like paying tax on my profit. After all, I need all of my cash for reinvestment. That's where the 1031 Tax-Deferred Exchange comes in handy. Here's how it works.

Section 1031 Tax-Deferred Exchange

Under this special circumstance, investors are permitted to exchange one property for another, reinvest all monies and profits from it and defer the tax on the capital gain until a later date. Consider the 1031 Exchange a Congressional gift to investors. Only business and investment properties will qualify for 1031 Exchange, not your personal residence. It is important to note that the properties to be exchanged must be of "like kind"; that is, you cannot trade a mortgage note for a double. However, you are permitted to trade one double as down payment on two doubles, or trade ten doubles towards a more expensive apartment complex.

The keys to the success of this tactic are to trade up without receiving any money at closing and to abide by the deadlines. Since the law outlining the exchange process has very specific requirements, be certain that you receive competent professional advice before you agree to an exchange.

The simplest form of exchange is the two-party exchange. Owner A exchanges his rental property for rental property owned by B. But finding another investor who is willing to trade with you at that moment is anything but simple. Far more common is the three-party exchange, where two of the three participants own rental property, while the third brings money into the transaction. Two of the three leave the transaction with rental property; the third leaves with cash and/or notes.

If you are one of the participants of the three-way exchange and have not had time to locate a property to exchange into, IRS allows delayed exchanges, provided certain conditions are met. For example, in your sale documents, you must specifically state your intention of engaging in a 1031 exchange. Your escrow closing agent will keep a copy and you should ask for a copy for your records. When the sale of your property takes place, the escrow agent will place the funds that you would ordinarily receive into an escrow account. From the time your property is sold, you have 45 days to inform that agent of the property you wish to purchase, and 180 days from that same date of sale to close your new deal. Since tax laws are frequently rewritten, it would be wise to check with your tax lawyer or accountant for any changes that will affect your transaction.

With a 1031 Exchange, you can defer the depreciation and profit you've realized on the properties you wish to sell. It can be an excellent tactic for investors who want to build up their portfolio of rental properties by reinvesting all cash sums from sales. So rather than following the "Buy, Sell, and Pay Tax" scenario, consider this one: "Buy, Sell, and Trade!"

Rehabilitation Tax Credits

A number of years ago, there were accelerated depreciation schedules for low-income housing. These have been replaced with Low-Income Housing Tax Credits. The tax credits are state allocated but federally mandated and, once received, can be used for 10 years. They are not tax deductions, like depreciation, for example, which you are allowed to subtract from your income before calculating the amount of income tax you owe. Instead these are actual tax credits that are subtracted at the end of your tax form, after the tax amount due has been calculated. In other words, these credits reduce your tax burden dollar for dollar. It is quite possible, for example, to receive a tax credit for $2,000 for 10 years. That means, in actuality, you would receive $20,000 on one double alone! Moreover, you can still take all of your usual deductions for repairs and depreciation.

The purpose of this program is to reward the investor who provides and improves inner-city property for low-income individuals or families. Typical "old-school" slumlords need not apply. To qualify, your projects must be of historical significance or must provide housing for low-income tenants. You must spend a minimum of $3,000 per unit on repairs alone. The more you spend on rehabilitation, the larger the tax credit allowed. Now you understand another reason why I install new roofs and furnaces so frequently. Providing you do a very thorough job, that is, spend plenty of money on a vacant project, you may be able to get an additional credit for 40% of the purchase price as well.

Although this is my favorite tax loophole, it has its drawbacks. For one thing, these credits are not always available, so you'd be wise to check with your state housing agency to find out if funds are currently on hand. A second drawback is the paperwork involved. It is complex and often difficult to complete to the satisfaction of the state housing finance agency. Your best approach is to contact the housing agency in your state and ask for an application and information packet. If seminars are offered, to educate you on the ins and outs of the paperwork, I recommend that you attend one or all of them.

State housing agencies are not always easy to locate, since they are called different names in each state. Housing Finance Commission, Housing Development Office, and Development Finance Authority are just three of the many variations. If your state government telephone information operator is not able to help you, call the National Council of State Housing Agencies at (202) 624-7710. Their staff can direct you to the housing agency in your state.

Stay in Touch with Your Taxes

I prepare my own tax returns, since I want to stay thoroughly in touch with all aspects of my business. I advise all investors to do the same. But that doesn't mean that you should shy away from professional help. Seek tax advice from the experts and learn from it. Periodically, make an appointment with a good real estate accountant for spot checks. Take your completed tax forms in, for a good review and critique. For the specific questions that pop up from time to time, ask your accountant or the Internal Revenue Service. Request free publications from IRS and purchase tax information books from office supply stores or bookstores to keep you well informed. Discuss tax questions with other landlords.

Take time to keep accurate records. Save all purchase receipts for materials and labor used on each property, even a cash receipt for an 89-cent key. File your receipts appropriately, in a well-organized fashion.

Since you're in the investment business to make money, you'll want to be able to write off every expense at tax time. As long as you keep buying and improving real estate, you will provide an ongoing tax shelter for yourself. The problem arises when you stop spending large amounts of money on repairs. In my case, it pays to install new furnaces, carpet, and other large ticket items. The government encourages me to do so.

I am amazed at the number of people who believe that the government has stifled investors. In fact, it's those who hold high-powered jobs who suffer when income taxes are raised and when loopholes are closed; there is no where else for them to turn. But for every loophole the government closes to the working wealthy, they seem to open a new one for me. In my real estate investment business, it seems the harder I work, the "luckier" I get.

Part VIII
One Landlord's
Perspective

14

One Landlord's Perspective

Recently, at a social gathering, someone commented to me, "I heard that you're in the rehab business." For a moment, I was caught off guard. I've never considered this to be my actual profession. I think of myself in the apartment rental business. Rehabilitation is secondary. It's a very small part of what I do; in fact, I rehab only when I acquire another property. As you know, my primary goal is to own rental housing and to manage it efficiently and profitably. The word "rehab" suggests that this is my end goal, and it also suggests that I work for other property owners as well. Frankly, while I would do this kind of work for myself, I have no desire to do it for anyone else. I am a business owner, but I am not above manual labor when I can see that it is saving me money on my units and cutting my costs to increase my cash flow.

When I'm not in the acquisition phase, I may go for many weeks just working a half-day per week in the field, spending time also on paperwork in my home office. Other landlords are not as fortunate. I have learned the value of maintenance and improvements to my properties, the art of keeping them in excellent condition so that I won't be called out at inconvenient times. While I am willing to work long, hard hours when it is necessary to bring me closer to my goal— especially when there are vacancies or new properties to work on— I certainly enjoy the freedom that this business gives me.

Dressed for Success

At first it was difficult for me to accept the fact that, no matter how financially prosperous I became, I would never fit society's classic image of a successful business-man. Dusty jeans and a well-worn jacket certainly do not call to mind the phrase "executive income." Surprisingly, it was hard for me to realize that even though I had reached a high level of success, I couldn't dress the part. Then I met the elderly multimillionaire I mentioned earlier in the book, the man who drove an old truck and wore a shoe with a hole in it. He and I were in the same line of work, but his attire was in far worse shape than mine and so was his vehicle. But he was an even greater success! This man inspired me in many ways. After I got to know him, I found it easier to dress down for work.

Along with my change in wardrobe, I eventually gave up my vision of working in a plush downtown office, with a sports car to get me there. While that vision was possible when I worked in sales jobs, I found little satisfaction in that type of work. Not only was the pay never quite high enough, but I was always working for someone else, selling someone else's product. I realized that my education at The Ohio State University would not help me get a better position because I had not graduated. The only career that could bring me executive income without further education was real estate. Now, after years in the business, I know that I made the right decision. The executive income is there, all right, and I savor the pleasure of being my own boss.

Expand Your Business When the Mood Hits

Now that I have a basic portfolio of buildings, expansion comes in mood swings. I can go for two years and not buy one property, because I feel that I have sufficient cash reserves and income. Then, out of the blue, I get fired up again and want to own the whole thoroughfare that runs through my investment district. Right now, I'm in the midst of an acquisition phase again, with a renewed desire to double my holdings and income.

As I mentioned in the early pages of this book, I think of each property as a part-time job. When you have taken on enough part-time jobs to equal the income that suits your needs, stop expanding. When you want a pay increase, either buy another property or simply raise the rents. You'll get "raises", too, at other times. Whenever you pay off a mortgage loan, for instance, you'll experience an immediate increase in pay. If you have twenty units and raise rents by $25, for example, your income will increase by $500 per month. If you own forty units, you'll raise your monthly income by $1000 a month and so on. I use the figure of 20 units because this should be your initial target. The acquisition of twenty units (ten doubles) will allow you to begin tasting success and consider quitting that "real" job. Forty units (twenty doubles) lets you move to that expensive house in the suburbs.

Be Realistic About Your Equity Position

When I buy a new rental property, I don't fool myself into thinking that I have "instant equity", as you'll hear so often on late-night television. Sounds glamorous! But be realistic; the only equity I have "instantly" is my down payment. However, as I make repairs and improvements at nominal cost, my equity position is increased, beyond the actual repair expenses. For example, if my new roof costs $600 and everyone else pays $3,200, then my equity is strengthened by $3,200. Also, if my exterior paint job costs $600 and everyone else pays $1,900, then I have increased my equity position by $1,900. The transformation of this run-down property into a higher money-making investment will therefore increase my equity position.

As the mortgage loan is paid down, the equity will continue to build, even if the market value of the property does not increase. You'll note that equity position is based on the going market price for the property at that particular time. In other words, the property is only worth what someone will pay. So be realistic when you calculate your equity; don't expect a down payment of

$2,000 to yield you an instant equity of $15,000. In this business, you can't afford not to be a realist.

Your Ever-Increasing Cash Flow

The short-term financing that I recommend for your investment property will, in a few years, provide substantial boosts to your cash flow. As you pay off the loan on several of your buildings, the increases in your monthly income will be considerable.

This is a wonderful way to eliminate all your retirement concerns as well. Here's how my "retirement plan" works. As the years go by, the rents on your units will gradually be increased, while your mortgage payment remains the same. (You won't be refinancing to draw cash from your properties.) As an example, you may decide to raise the monthly rent on your double every three years, by $25 per unit. After eight years, your short-term loan has been paid off and that brings an end to your monthly principal and interest payment of $250. At the nine-year mark, your income is much higher than it was originally. The two units yield a total of $150 extra per month and now that the loan is paid off, you have freed up an additional $250. For the rest of your life, you can continue to raise the rents and never again have a mortgage loan payment to make. This is my idea of the perfect retirement plan. Can you imagine what it would be like to have dozens of these "retirement plans", all working for you?

In the very near future, I will have paid off a group of mortgages with payments totaling $1,700 per month. The $1,700 will then be added into my current monthly cash flow. What a pay raise! I doubt if I worked any harder than you did over the last few years. Have you had that substantial a pay raise lately? It's only one of many that I've had in recent years, with more to come in the future. When you're considering your retirement plan, don't forget about the 15- and 30-year notes (and even shorter ones with balloons) you may receive when you finance property that you're selling. All of these can increase your retirement income greatly.

Here's a Truly Permanent Part-time Job

I've noticed an interesting phenomenon about this particular business. Once you own property and get your little "part-time job" in place, it is set for your lifetime. One of my doubles, paid off, nets at the very least $137.50 a week. If you consider that I don't even have to appear on the jobsite for more than a moment once or twice a month, I'm sure you'll agree that it's a pretty good part-time job. I simply maintain the building and see that it remains rented. Once my properties are set, I'm set.

Other business owners cannot make the same claims. Can they sleep in or go shopping tomorrow and still make the same amount of money? Most cannot. They must continue to make contacts and court new clients, for without them, their business would die. In my previous sales jobs, I put together the sale, received a commission, and then the job was finished. Tomorrow was always a new day with new clients. To me, it seemed like a job with no future and certainly no security. There was no accumulation of benefits from my labors; each day I started over. However, in my business, what I did yesterday builds my permanent income for the future.

Think about your situation: your job, your responsibilities, your income, your wealth accumulation program, and your retirement plan. Does your job require you to stay on the run, developing contacts with new clients or customers, week in and week out? Do your responsibilities increase, while your income treads water? Does your present job allow you to increase your income whenever you need or want to? Are you able to accumulate wealth? Finally, will your I.R.A. or other retirement plan provide enough income for you when you leave your job? If you're not satisfied with your answers to these questions, then this may be the time to make a change. Streetwise investing in rental housing may be your dream opportunity.

When I'm asked, "If it's that easy, why doesn't everybody do it?", my reply is simple: "It **isn't** that easy. That's why not many people do it." If you've read the entire book, you realize that real estate investing can be both difficult and discouraging at times. There is a great deal to learn and, as you work your way through the learning process, you'll find that there's an art to buying, repairing, renting, and selling. But once you've mastered the techniques, you'll find great satisfaction and fulfillment in putting it all together successfully. Although I'm fond of saying, "The harder I work, the luckier I get", in reality, you must make the luck happen by working hard, doing the best job that you possibly can, and thereby making good things happen for yourself.

Your Contribution to Your Community

When you follow my strategy for owning and managing rental housing, you'll find that you are, at the same time, making a valuable contribution to society. Granted, your initial goal is to provide yourself and your family with a high standard of living. You want to establish for yourself a job and an income that are secure, with no worries about being laid off or fired. But while you're carrying out your dream, you'll have the additional satisfaction of knowing that your tenants and your community as a whole benefit with every building that you undertake.

How much of a contribution you will make may not be immediately apparent. But when you see the conditions under which many low-income people are forced to live because better housing is not available to them, you'll understand exactly what I mean.

In my units, tenants are provided with apartments that measure up to the city code standards. That sounds like a simple statement, but it often takes many repairs to make that claim. Although all of my properties are in excellent condition when I sell them, I have never once purchased a property like this. Most of the buildings I have bought over the years had a whole host of violations, both large and small, and yet tenants lived there, in spite of the substandard conditions.

All of my new tenants move into a clean and safe environment. Naturally, I don't install the best cabinetry, nor do I lay the best linoleum. But measured improvements are made, even to the smallest detail. Everything is in working condition. By the time I've finished my initial renovations, my properties are the most attractive in the neighborhood, inside and out.

For most of the tenants I rent to, this is the first opportunity they've had to move into an apartment with new carpet and a new high-efficiency furnace. It may sound unbelievable to you, but I assure you it is certainly true. Most of my tenants appreciate living in a well-cared-for unit and they, in turn, maintain it nicely. As I discussed earlier, there are the occasional bad tenants, of course, who do not respect anything. But if they are unwilling to keep the unit clean and neat, they won't be renting from you for long. It gives me great pleasure to rent to families, especially where there are children who will enjoy a better quality of life because I've offered them a decent place to live. Children, in particular, are delighted to have nicer bedrooms, with ceiling lights that work and a furnace that provides adequate heat to their bedrooms.

When you initially purchase your buildings, you may be astounded at the current living condition some families must tolerate, because there is no other choice. I once bought a double where, in the bathroom, the toilet was stopped up, there was no washbasin, and the water lines to the bathtub were cut off. Two families lived here. The tenants had complained for many weeks, but because they were afraid of losing even this, they had not called the city inspector for fear of landlord retribution. Naturally, even before the closing (with the seller's permission), I got the bathroom in full working order. Normally I wait until I actually own the building, but this situation was so serious, I didn't want the deed transferred into my name with violations like that.

In making the repairs to badly abused buildings, I am simply conducting my business as it should be. Fortunately what is best for my business happens to also be best for my tenants. They benefit from living in a cleaner and safer environment. I benefit from a profitable business, but I also receive, as an extra benefit, satisfaction from seeing my tenants in better surroundings.

When I appear at one of my properties in the summertime, to paint the exterior, you'd be surprised at the subtle, but conspicuous, response. Neighbors will work in their gardens, mow their lawns, and trim hedges. More noticeably, other properties begin to be painted and fixed up. Following my lead, other owners start to see the advantage in increasing the value of their properties. Soon the whole neighborhood looks better. I recently painted a double and the next week, three other properties were painted as well. When I help myself by improving my property, I often find that my neighbors help me by painting their houses. In the end, we all benefit. The neighborhood is gradually revitalized, and property values rise. I remember long ago when my furnace contractor remarked that I had single-handedly changed the complexion of the neighborhood. Of course, he was teasing. I was only the impetus that set the property owners into action. Now I am just one of the participants in an overall effort to renew the neighborhood.

While I have not made earth-shaking changes to our society, I have, nevertheless improved lives of individuals and families, and improved the appearance of neighborhoods as well. Yes, I have evicted druggies and nonpays. But those tenants who abide by the law and pay their rent can find in my units a good, clean residence managed by a fair and honest landlord. If their next door neighbor engages in illegal activities and also lives in one of my units, my good tenants can rest assured that I will contact the police. I consider it my responsibility to provide a peaceful and pleasant environment for my tenants. This improves the neighborhood and, indirectly, helps society as a whole.

Giving People a Second Chance

I rent to anyone with rent and deposit. When prospective tenants call to ask if my units are available, they often ask if a credit check is required. I can usually hear them breathe a sigh of relief when I answer "No."

In my business, there are no credit rejects. Everyone gets the opportunity to rent from me. As you recall, homeless agencies call me, and I place their clients into my apartments, even though I know that most of these tenants have been evicted from their previous apartments for nonpayment of rent. These are the people who find themselves set out on the street, with nowhere to go. These agencies with church money take them in on a temporary basis and attempt to find them housing. They wear out the Sunday paper calling around to get them relocated so that they can quickly get these families back into the mainstream of society. If families remain homeless too long, the agencies fear that it will be virtually impossible for these folks to function as a normal family ever again.

This situation works as well for me, the landlord, as it does for the tenants and the agencies offering assistance. I want my units filled as soon as they are ready and I insist upon full rent and deposit. If I call and give the agency a list of vacancies, very often they will provide me with a tenant, the rent and the deposit. My units are filled quickly with someone who usually appreciates the favor of a second chance. And again, as I help myself, not only does the family benefit, but society benefits as well.

Sharing My Strategy for Success

I have written this book and shared my investment strategy with you for several reasons. First, I admit that I'm proud of what I have accomplished and I get tremendous enjoyment out of showing others how they, too, can create their own job, as I did. I want to save other investors the long period of trial and error that's inevitable without a well-defined, well-tested strategy to follow. I want to help other landlords find solutions to their problems, answers that are often not readily available to them in the often-isolated life landlords lead.

It has concerned me that the "real estate televangelists" have not only glorified the business of real estate investment but have distorted it as well. Bad real estate advice is particularly dangerous. I want would-be investors to have an honest and accurate account of the business of owning rental housing. They'll benefit and society will benefit when investors are knowledgeable and street-smart.

If you are dissatisfied with your life and think more highly of yourself than what the cards have dealt you, I hope that I can help you and your family reach a higher plateau of success in life. By putting into practice the advice that I've shared with you in these pages, I hope that you, too, can raise the standard of living for many families who've never had an opportunity to know decent housing; you, too, can assist in the rehabilitation of a neighborhood. It's simply good business.

Part IX
Appendix

Glossary

Balloon Payment: A final lump-sum payment of the balance due on a note, to be paid on or before a date that is specified in the note. For example, on a note with a 3-year balloon, the borrower must pay off the entire existing loan balance three years after the note is signed.

Capital gain: The amount of taxable profit realized when a property is sold. An amount equal to the sales price of the property (less selling expenses) minus the adjusted tax basis.

Cash flow: The investor's profit from rents received, after all expenses and debt service have been paid.

Chain-investing: Leveraging; the investor borrows from a property he already owns to purchase another property. By obtaining a loan on the second property, a third can be purchased, and so on.

Depreciation: A federal income tax deduction based on a percentage of the value of an investment property, business equipment and vehicles.

Double: A two-family dwelling with side-by-side units; a side-by-side duplex.

Duplex: A two-family dwelling; in some areas, the word "duplex" indicates a two-storey building with one living unit above the other.

Equity: An amount equal to the value of the property minus the balance owed on loans secured by the property.

Free and clear: Without debt; a property is said to be owned "free and clear" if there are no loans against it.

Land sales contract: A type of seller-financing agreement. Also known as land contract or contract for deed.

Leveraging: See "Chain-investing."

Lien check: A service offered by some title insurance companies, providing the name of the owner, mortgage and lien information about a property.

Market rent: Average rent charged directly to tenant in the open market, without government participation.

Multiple listing service: A service that provides a listing of properties for sale in a community, for the use of real estate agents who subscribe to this service. Usually published in book form or computer data file.

Portfolio: Property owned by an investor; includes real estate and/or notes.

Purchase money mortgage (PMM): A security device often used in seller-financing transactions, where the seller owns the property free and clear, then agrees to carry a first mortgage.

Reality assist: See "Lien check": Similar to a lien check but this is a service provided to real estate agents only, often at no charge or a reduced fee.

Redlining: An illegal practice in which lending institutions refuse to make loans on properties in certain undesirable areas.

Rate of return: The percentage of profit received on the money that is invested. Calculated by dividing the cash flow by the amount invested, on either a monthly, annual or overall ownership basis. Conservative or aggressive calculations can be determined by using actual or projected figures.

Rehabilitation tax credit: A federal income tax credit granted to investors who spend a designated amount of money in upgrading housing for low-income tenants. This is not simply a deduction, but an actual credit, allowing the investor to substitute a "credit dollar" for a "tax dollar" that is owed.

Return on investment: See "Rate of return."

Section 8: A federal program administered through local metropolitan housing agencies; a partial or full rent check is mailed directly to landlords for approved low-income families.

Section 1031 tax-deferred exchange: A loophole for investors whereby taxes on capital gain may be deferred by trading like-kind property.

Streamlined refinance without appraisal: A refinance available to holders of VA and FHA loans on investment properties, without typical application procedures and expense. Properties must have been owned for at least six months, with loan payments made on time.

Weasel clause: An escape clause in an offer to purchase that enables the buyer or seller to back out of the deal without legal repercussion. "Contingent upon approval" or "contingent upon inspection" are two common weasel clauses.

Amortization Chart

U se this chart to determine what your monthly principal and interest payment will be. Real estate loan payments are amortized over the term of the loan. That is, the payments are calculated to include the correct amount of principal and interest so that the loan balance will be zero at the end of the term.

Step 1: Find the applicable interest rate in the top row.

Step 2: Find the term of the loan in the column on the left.

Step 3: Trace down the rate column and across the term row to the square where the two meet. Remember this factor.

Step 4: Move the decimal point in your loan amount three places to the left.

Example: $57,850. becomes 57.850.

Step 5: Multiply this number by the factor found on the chart.

Example: A 10% loan with a term of 30 years would have a factor of 8.78 according to the chart. If the loan balance is $57,850, we would multiply 57.850 by 8.78 and find that our monthly payment (principal and interest) would be $507.92.

Appendix II: Amortization Chart

YEAR	8.50	8.25	8.00	7.75	7.50	7.25	7.00	6.75	6.50	6.25	6.00	5.75	5.50	5.25	5.00	4.75	4.50	4.25	4.00
1	87.22	87.10	86.99	86.87	86.76	86.64	86.53	86.41	86.30	86.18	86.07	85.95	85.84	85.72	85.61	85.49	85.38	85.26	85.15
2	45.46	45.34	45.23	45.11	45.00	44.89	44.77	44.66	44.55	44.43	44.32	44.21	44.10	43.98	43.87	43.76	43.65	43.54	43.42
3	31.57	31.45	31.34	31.22	31.11	30.99	30.88	30.76	30.65	30.54	30.42	30.31	30.20	30.08	29.97	29.86	29.75	29.64	29.52
4	24.65	24.53	24.41	24.30	24.18	24.06	23.95	23.83	23.71	23.60	23.49	23.37	23.26	23.14	23.03	22.92	22.80	22.69	22.58
5	20.52	20.40	20.28	20.16	20.04	19.92	19.80	19.68	19.57	19.45	19.33	19.22	19.10	18.99	18.87	18.76	18.64	18.53	18.42
6	17.78	17.66	17.53	17.41	17.29	17.17	17.05	16.93	16.81	16.69	16.57	16.46	16.34	16.22	16.10	15.99	15.87	15.76	15.65
7	15.84	15.71	15.59	15.46	15.34	15.22	15.09	14.97	14.85	14.73	14.61	14.49	14.37	14.25	14.13	14.02	13.90	13.78	13.67
8	14.39	14.26	14.14	14.01	13.88	13.76	13.63	13.51	13.39	13.26	13.14	13.02	12.90	12.78	12.66	12.54	12.42	12.31	12.19
9	13.28	13.15	13.02	12.89	12.76	12.63	12.51	12.38	12.25	12.13	12.01	11.88	11.76	11.64	11.52	11.40	11.28	11.16	11.04
10	12.40	12.27	12.13	12.00	11.87	11.74	11.61	11.48	11.35	11.23	11.10	10.98	10.85	10.73	10.61	10.48	10.36	10.24	10.12
11	11.69	11.55	11.42	11.28	11.15	11.02	10.88	10.75	10.62	10.49	10.37	10.24	10.11	9.99	9.86	9.74	9.62	9.50	9.38
12	11.10	10.96	10.82	10.69	10.55	10.42	10.28	10.15	10.02	9.89	9.76	9.63	9.50	9.37	9.25	9.12	9.00	8.88	8.76
13	10.61	10.47	10.33	10.19	10.05	9.92	9.78	9.65	9.51	9.38	9.25	9.12	8.99	8.86	8.73	8.60	8.48	8.35	8.23
14	10.20	10.06	9.91	9.77	9.63	9.49	9.35	9.22	9.08	8.95	8.81	8.68	8.55	8.42	8.29	8.16	8.03	7.91	7.78
15	9.85	9.70	9.56	9.41	9.27	9.13	8.99	8.85	8.71	8.57	8.44	8.30	8.17	8.04	7.91	7.78	7.65	7.52	7.40
16	9.54	9.40	9.25	9.10	8.96	8.81	8.67	8.53	8.39	8.25	8.11	7.98	7.84	7.71	7.58	7.45	7.32	7.19	7.06
17	9.28	9.13	8.98	8.83	8.69	8.54	8.40	8.25	8.11	7.97	7.83	7.69	7.56	7.42	7.29	7.15	7.02	6.89	6.76
18	9.05	8.90	8.75	8.60	8.45	8.30	8.16	8.01	7.87	7.72	7.58	7.44	7.30	7.17	7.03	6.90	6.76	6.63	6.50
19	8.85	8.70	8.55	8.39	8.24	8.09	7.94	7.79	7.65	7.50	7.36	7.22	7.08	6.94	6.80	6.67	6.53	6.40	6.27
20	8.68	8.52	8.36	8.21	8.06	7.90	7.75	7.60	7.46	7.31	7.16	7.02	6.88	6.74	6.60	6.46	6.33	6.19	6.06
21	8.52	8.36	8.20	8.05	7.89	7.74	7.58	7.43	7.28	7.14	6.99	6.84	6.70	6.56	6.42	6.28	6.14	6.01	5.87
22	8.38	8.22	8.06	7.90	7.75	7.59	7.43	7.28	7.13	6.98	6.83	6.68	6.54	6.39	6.25	6.11	5.97	5.84	5.70
23	8.26	8.10	7.93	7.77	7.61	7.46	7.30	7.14	6.99	6.84	6.69	6.54	6.39	6.25	6.10	5.96	5.82	5.68	5.55
24	8.15	7.98	7.82	7.66	7.50	7.34	7.18	7.02	6.87	6.71	6.56	6.41	6.26	6.11	5.97	5.83	5.68	5.54	5.41
25	8.05	7.88	7.72	7.55	7.39	7.23	7.07	6.91	6.75	6.60	6.44	6.29	6.14	5.99	5.85	5.70	5.56	5.42	5.28
26	7.96	7.79	7.63	7.46	7.29	7.13	6.97	6.81	6.65	6.49	6.34	6.18	6.03	5.88	5.73	5.59	5.44	5.30	5.16
27	7.88	7.71	7.54	7.37	7.21	7.04	6.88	6.72	6.56	6.40	6.24	6.08	5.93	5.78	5.63	5.48	5.34	5.19	5.05
28	7.81	7.64	7.47	7.30	7.13	6.96	6.80	6.63	6.47	6.31	6.15	5.99	5.84	5.69	5.54	5.39	5.24	5.09	4.95
29	7.75	7.57	7.40	7.23	7.06	6.89	6.72	6.56	6.39	6.23	6.07	5.91	5.76	5.60	5.45	5.30	5.15	5.00	4.86
30	7.69	7.51	7.34	7.16	6.99	6.82	6.65	6.49	6.32	6.16	6.00	5.84	5.68	5.52	5.37	5.22	5.07	4.92	4.77

YEAR	8.75	9.00	9.25	9.50	9.75	10.00	10.25	10.50	10.75	11.00	11.25	11.50	11.75	12.00	12.25	12.50	12.75	13.00
1	87.34	87.45	87.57	87.68	87.80	87.92	88.03	88.15	88.27	88.38	88.50	88.62	88.73	88.85	88.97	89.08	89.20	89.32
	45.57	45.68	45.80	45.91	46.03	46.14	46.26	46.38	46.49	46.61	46.72	46.84	46.96	47.07	47.19	47.31	47.42	47.54
	31.68	31.80	31.92	32.03	32.15	32.27	32.38	32.50	32.62	32.74	32.86	32.98	33.10	33.21	33.33	33.45	33.57	33.69
	24.77	24.89	25.00	25.12	25.24	25.36	25.48	25.60	25.72	25.85	25.97	26.09	26.21	26.33	26.46	26.58	26.70	26.83
5	20.64	20.76	20.88	21.00	21.12	21.25	21.37	21.49	21.62	21.74	21.87	21.99	22.12	22.24	22.37	22.50	22.63	22.75
	17.90	18.03	18.15	18.27	18.40	18.53	18.65	18.78	18.91	19.03	19.16	19.29	19.42	19.55	19.68	19.81	19.94	20.07
	15.96	16.09	16.22	16.34	16.47	16.60	16.73	16.86	16.99	17.12	17.25	17.39	17.52	17.65	17.79	17.92	18.06	18.19
	14.52	14.65	14.78	14.91	15.04	15.17	15.31	15.44	15.57	15.71	15.84	15.98	16.12	16.25	16.39	16.53	16.67	16.81
	13.41	13.54	13.68	13.81	13.94	14.08	14.21	14.35	14.49	14.63	14.76	14.90	15.04	15.18	15.33	15.47	15.61	15.75
10	12.53	12.67	12.80	12.94	13.08	13.22	13.35	13.49	13.63	13.78	13.92	14.06	14.20	14.35	14.49	14.64	14.78	14.93
	11.82	11.96	12.10	12.24	12.38	12.52	12.66	12.80	12.95	13.09	13.24	13.38	13.53	13.68	13.83	13.98	14.13	14.28
	11.24	11.38	11.52	11.66	11.81	11.95	12.10	12.24	12.39	12.54	12.68	12.83	12.98	13.13	13.29	13.44	13.59	13.75
	10.75	10.90	11.04	11.19	11.33	11.48	11.63	11.78	11.92	12.08	12.23	12.38	12.53	12.69	12.84	13.00	13.15	13.31
	10.34	10.49	10.64	10.78	10.93	11.08	11.23	11.38	11.54	11.69	11.85	12.00	12.16	12.31	12.47	12.63	12.79	12.95
15	9.99	10.14	10.29	10.44	10.59	10.75	10.90	11.05	11.21	11.37	11.52	11.68	11.84	12.00	12.16	12.33	12.49	12.65
	9.69	9.85	10.00	10.15	10.30	10.46	10.62	10.77	10.93	11.09	11.25	11.41	11.57	11.74	11.90	12.07	12.23	12.40
	9.43	9.59	9.74	9.90	10.05	10.21	10.37	10.53	10.69	10.85	11.02	11.18	11.35	11.51	11.68	11.85	12.02	12.19
	9.21	9.36	9.52	9.68	9.84	10.00	10.16	10.32	10.49	10.65	10.82	10.98	11.15	11.32	11.49	11.66	11.83	12.00
	9.01	9.17	9.33	9.49	9.65	9.81	9.98	10.14	10.31	10.47	10.64	10.81	10.98	11.15	11.33	11.50	11.67	11.85
20	8.84	9.00	9.16	9.32	9.49	9.65	9.82	9.98	10.15	10.32	10.49	10.66	10.84	11.01	11.19	11.36	11.54	11.72
	8.68	8.85	9.01	9.17	9.34	9.51	9.68	9.85	10.02	10.19	10.36	10.54	10.71	10.89	11.06	11.24	11.42	11.60
	8.55	8.71	8.88	9.04	9.21	9.38	9.55	9.73	9.90	10.07	10.25	10.42	10.60	10.78	10.96	11.14	11.32	11.50
	8.43	8.59	8.76	8.93	9.10	9.27	9.44	9.62	9.79	9.97	10.15	10.33	10.51	10.69	10.87	11.05	11.23	11.42
	8.32	8.49	8.66	8.83	9.00	9.17	9.35	9.52	9.70	9.88	10.06	10.24	10.42	10.60	10.79	10.97	11.16	11.34
25	8.22	8.39	8.56	8.74	8.91	9.09	9.26	9.44	9.62	9.80	9.98	10.16	10.35	10.53	10.72	10.90	11.09	11.28
	8.13	8.31	8.48	8.66	8.83	9.01	9.19	9.37	9.55	9.73	9.91	10.10	10.28	10.47	10.66	10.84	11.03	11.22
	8.06	8.23	8.41	8.58	8.76	8.94	9.12	9.30	9.49	9.67	9.85	10.04	10.23	10.41	10.60	10.79	10.98	11.17
	7.99	8.16	8.34	8.52	8.70	8.88	9.06	9.25	9.43	9.61	9.80	9.99	10.18	10.37	10.56	10.75	10.94	11.13
	7.92	8.10	8.28	8.46	8.64	8.82	9.01	9.19	9.38	9.57	9.75	9.94	10.13	10.32	10.52	10.71	10.90	11.09
30	7.87	8.05	8.23	8.41	8.59	8.78	8.96	9.15	9.33	9.52	9.71	9.90	10.09	10.29	10.48	10.67	10.87	11.06

YEAR

INDEX

ABOUT THE AUTHOR

A native of Columbus, Ohio, H. Roger Neal has built a very succesful business there. While he was a student at The Ohio State University, he first envisioned a plan of owning and managing rental housing. For several years after he purchased his first investment property, he continued to hold a regular job while fulfilling his dream of expanding his portfolio of properties. His determination, hard work and hands-on approach paid off and his business grew.

Over the years, the author has developed and refined his investment strategy to include the well-tested tips and techniques he writes about in this book. Now president of the Real Estate Investors' Association of Columbus, and vice-president of the Ohio Real Estate Investors' Association, he is a member of the Columbus Board of Realtors.

For information about H. Roger Neal's real estate newsletter, plus audio and software products for advanced investors, readers are invited to contact Myriad Publishing, Inc., P.O.Box 1109, Dublin, OH 43017-1109, (800) 427-1072.

New Releases from
The Panoply Press Real Estate Series

First Home Buying Guide
by H.L. Kibbey
New Fifth Edition of this popular bestseller.
The complete guide for the first-time homebuyer gives a step-by-step plan for researching the market, choosing a loan, buying a home.
ISBN 1-882877-04-7   160 pages, softcover $10.95

Streetwise Investing in Rental Housing
by H. Roger Neal
A detailed strategy for financial independence, this book offers a sound and sensible approach to owning and managing rental housing.
ISBN 1-882877-03-9   240 pages, softcover $15.95

The Growing-Older Guide to Real Estate
by H.L. Kibbey
What everyone over 50 should know about buying, selling, financing and owning a home. Equity conversion, tax considerations, buying and selling tips for stress-free real estate decisions. National award-winning book by the host of House Calls.
ISBN 0-9615067-8-4   192 pages, softcover $14.95

How to Finance a Home in the Pacific Northwest
by H.L. Kibbey
New Third Edition of this two-time national award-winner. The complete guide for financing and refinancing in Oregon and Washington state.
ISBN 1-882877-09-8   240 pages, softcover $15.95

Appeal Your Property Taxes — and Win
by Ed Salzman
Learn what it takes to cut your tax bill. Insider's secrets from an appeals expert gives state-by-state guidelines for a winning appeal.
ISBN 1-882877-01-2   128 pages, softcover $9.95

Panoply Press books are available at bookstores everywhere. If you're unable to find any of these titles, they may be ordered by mail from the publisher, Panoply Press, Inc. Please enclose your check or money order for the cost of the books plus $3.50 shipping per order.

PANOPLY PRESS, INC.
P.O. Box 1885
Lake Oswego, OR 97035
(503) 697-7964   (800) 826-6579

What other investors have said about the book:

"H. Roger Neal has a unique way of approaching the time-tested wealth-building possibilities of real estate investment. Streetwise Investing in Rental Housing will be the most dog-eared volume in your personal real estate library."

Vena Jones-Cox
Host of "Real-Life Real Estate"

"I admit to being a sceptic when I first read Neal's book, since I live in an area of very high priced housing. But it really works!! Great strategy!"

Loren Jenkins
Investor, Mountain View, CA

"I was delighted and impressed with "Streetwise Investing". It's a road map that shows how ANYONE can become financially independent in the largest industry in America-- Rental Housing."

Sue Brawn,
Former Board Member,
National Real Estate Investors Association, Inc.